T3-BSD-992

BUDDHIST MONASTIC TRADITIONS OF SOUTHERN ASIA

BDK English Tripiṭaka 93-I

BUDDHIST MONASTIC TRADITIONS OF SOUTHERN ASIA

A RECORD OF THE INNER LAW SENT HOME FROM THE SOUTH SEAS

by

Śramaṇa Yijing

Translated from the Chinese
(Taishō Volume 54, Number 2125)

by

Li Rongxi

**Numata Center
for Buddhist Translation and Research
2000**

BQ
6065
.I183
N3613
2000

© 2000 by Bukkyō Dendō Kyōkai and
Numata Center for Buddhist Translation and Research

All rights reserved. No part of this book may be reproduced, stored in a retrieval system, or transcribed in any form or by any means —electronic, mechanical, photocopying, recording, or otherwise— without the prior written permission of the publisher.

First Printing, 2000
ISBN: 1-886439-09-5
Library of Congress Catalog Card Number: 98-67122

Published by
Numata Center for Buddhist Translation and Research
2620 Warring Street
Berkeley, California 94704

Printed in the United States of America

45436715

A Message on the Publication of the English Tripiṭaka

The Buddhist canon is said to contain eighty-four thousand different teachings. I believe that this is because the Buddha's basic approach was to prescribe a different treatment for every spiritual ailment, much as a doctor prescribes a different medicine for every medical ailment. Thus his teachings were always appropriate for the particular suffering individual and for the time at which the teaching was given, and over the ages not one of his prescriptions has failed to relieve the suffering to which it was addressed.

Ever since the Buddha's Great Demise over twenty-five hundred years ago, his message of wisdom and compassion has spread throughout the world. Yet no one has ever attempted to translate the entire Buddhist canon into English throughout the history of Japan. It is my greatest wish to see this done and to make the translations available to the many English-speaking people who have never had the opportunity to learn about the Buddha's teachings.

Of course, it would be impossible to translate all of the Buddha's eighty-four thousand teachings in a few years. I have, therefore, had one hundred thirty-nine of the scriptural texts in the prodigious Taishō edition of the Chinese Buddhist canon selected for inclusion in the First Series of this translation project.

It is in the nature of this undertaking that the results are bound to be criticized. Nonetheless, I am convinced that unless someone takes it upon himself or herself to initiate this project, it will never be done. At the same time, I hope that an improved, revised edition will appear in the future.

It is most gratifying that, thanks to the efforts of more than a hundred Buddhist scholars from the East and the West, this monumental project has finally gotten off the ground. May the rays of the Wisdom of the Compassionate One reach each and every person in the world.

NUMATA Yehan
Founder of the English
Tripiṭaka Project

August 7, 1991

Editorial Foreword

In January 1982, Dr. NUMATA Yehan, the founder of the Bukkyō Dendō Kyōkai (Society for the Promotion of Buddhism), decided to begin the monumental task of translating the complete Taishō edition of the Chinese Tripiṭaka (Buddhist Canon) into the English language. Under his leadership, a special preparatory committee was organized in April 1982. By July of the same year, the Translation Committee of the English Tripiṭaka was officially convened.

The initial Committee consisted of the following members: (late) HANAYAMA Shōyū (Chairperson); BANDŌ Shōjun; ISHIGAMI Zennō; KAMATA Shigeo; KANAOKA Shūyū; MAYEDA Sengaku; NARA Yasuaki; SAYEKI Shinkō; (late) SHIOIRI Ryōtatsu; TAMARU Noriyoshi; (late) TAMURA Kwansei; URYŪZU Ryūshin; and YUYAMA Akira. Assistant members of the Committee were as follows: KANAZAWA Atsushi; WATANABE Shōgo; Rolf Giebel of New Zealand; and Rudy Smet of Belgium.

After holding planning meetings on a monthly basis, the Committee selected one hundred thirty-nine texts for the First Series of translations, an estimated one hundred printed volumes in all. The texts selected are not necessarily limited to those originally written in India but also include works written or composed in China and Japan. While the publication of the First Series proceeds, the texts for the Second Series will be selected from among the remaining works; this process will continue until all the texts, in Japanese as well as in Chinese, have been published.

Frankly speaking, it will take perhaps one hundred years or more to accomplish the English translation of the complete Chinese and Japanese texts, for they consist of thousands of works. Nevertheless, as Dr. NUMATA wished, it is the sincere hope of the Committee that this project will continue unto completion, even after all its present members have passed away.

It must be mentioned here that the final object of this project is not academic fulfillment but the transmission of the teaching of the

Buddha to the whole world in order to create harmony and peace among humankind. To that end, the translators have been asked to minimize the use of explanatory notes of the kind that are indispensable in academic texts, so that the attention of general readers will not be unduly distracted from the primary text. Also, a glossary of selected terms is appended to aid in understanding the text.

To my great regret, however, Dr. NUMATA passed away on May 5, 1994, at the age of ninety-seven, entrusting his son, Mr. NUMATA Toshihide, with the continuation and completion of the Translation Project. The Committee also lost its able and devoted Chairperson, Professor HANAYAMA Shōyū, on June 16, 1995, at the age of sixty-three. After these severe blows, the Committee elected me, Vice-President of Musashino Women's College, to be the Chair in October 1995. The Committee has renewed its determination to carry out the noble intention of Dr. NUMATA, under the leadership of Mr. NUMATA Toshihide.

The present members of the Committee are MAYEDA Sengaku (Chairperson), BANDŌ Shōjun, ISHIGAMI Zennō, ICHISHIMA Shōshin, KAMATA Shigeo, KANAOKA Shūyū, NARA Yasuaki, SAYEKI Shinkō, TAMARU Noriyoshi, URYŪZU Ryūshin, and YUYAMA Akira. Assistant members are WATANABE Shōgo and UEDA Noboro.

The Numata Center for Buddhist Translation and Research was established in November 1984, in Berkeley, California, U.S.A., to assist in the publication of the BDK English Tripiṭaka First Series. In December 1991, the Publication Committee was organized at the Numata Center, with Professor Philip Yampolsky as the Chairperson. To our sorrow, Professor Yampolsky passed away in July 1996, but thankfully Dr. Kenneth Inada is continuing the work as Chairperson. This text is the eighteenth volume to be published and distributed by the Numata Center. All of the remaining texts will be published under the supervision of this Committee, in close cooperation with the Translation Committee in Tokyo.

MAYEDA Sengaku
Chairperson
Translation Committee of
the BDK English Tripiṭaka

June 28, 1999

Publisher's Foreword

The Publication Committee works in close cooperation with the Editorial Committee of the BDK English Tripiṭaka in Tokyo, Japan. Since December 1991, it has operated from the Numata Center for Buddhist Translation and Research in Berkeley, California. Its principal mission is to oversee and facilitate the publication in English of selected texts from the one hundred-volume Taishō Edition of the Chinese Tripiṭaka, along with a few major influential Japanese Buddhist texts not in the Tripiṭaka. The list of selected texts is conveniently appended at the end of each volume. In the text itself, the Taishō Edition page and column designations are provided in the margins.

The Committee is committed to the task of publishing clear, readable English texts. It honors the deep faith, spirit, and concern of the late Reverend Doctor NUMATA Yehan to disseminate Buddhist teachings throughout the world.

In July 1996, the Committee unfortunately lost its valued Chairperson, Dr. Philip Yampolsky, who was a stalwart leader, trusted friend, and esteemed colleague. We follow in his shadow. In February 1997, I was appointed to guide the Committee in his place.

The Committee is charged with the normal duties of a publishing firm—general editing, formatting, copyediting, proofreading, indexing, and checking linguistic fidelity. The Committee members are Diane Ames, Eisho Nasu, Koh Nishiike, and the president and director of the Numata Center, Reverend Kiyoshi S. Yamashita.

Kenneth K. Inada
Chairperson
Publication Committee

June 28, 1999

Contents

Translator's Introduction

A Record of the Inner Law Sent Home from the South Seas (Nan-hai-ji-gui-nei-fa-zhuan), Taishō No. 2125, in four fascicles, was composed by Yijing while he was sojourning in Śrībhoja (Sumatra) on his return journey from India.

Yijing (635–713), surnamed Zhang before becoming a monk, was a native of Qi-zhou (present Li-cheng County in Shandong Province). He was admitted to the monkhood at the age of fourteen. While he was still a youth of eighteen, he cherished the desire to travel to India to study Buddhism. His wish was not fulfilled until he was thirty-seven years old, in the second year of Xian-heng (671), during the reign of Emperor Gao-zhong of the Tang dynasty. When he was living in retirement during the summer season at Yang-zhou in that year, he became acquainted with Feng Xiao-quan, the Governor-designate of Guang-zhou (in the present Guangxi Zhuang Autonomous Region), who was ready to proceed to take up his post in the south. After the conclusion of the summer retreat, Yijing traveled with the new governor as far as Guang-zhou, where, with the generous support of the mandarin, he was able to sail in a Persian ship to the South Seas and reach Śrībhoja after a voyage of less than twenty days. Having stayed in Śrībhoja for six months to study the Sanskrit language, Yijing resumed his journey via Malaya, Kaccha, and the Islands of the Naked (Nicobar Islands), and arrived at Tāmralipti (the Calcutta area) in East India in the second month of the fourth year of Xian-heng (673). He stayed there for another year to continue his study of Sanskrit before starting his pilgrimage to Nālandā and other holy sites in Central India.

After having visited such sacred places as Vulture Peak near Rājagṛha, Mahābodhi Monastery, the old residence of Vimalakīrti at Vaiśālī, Kuśinagara, and Deer Park, he climbed over Kukkuṭapāda Mountain and returned to Nālandā Monastery, where he settled down and lived for ten years to study and translate Buddhist texts under the guidance of Ratnasiṃha, a learned teacher of the time who resided at the monastery.

Bringing with him Sanskrit texts in more than five hundred thousand stanzas, which when translated into Chinese would amount to a thousand fascicles, he sailed from Tāmralipti on his return journey and arrived at Śrībhoja for the second time in the third year of Chui-gong (687). This time he stayed there till he returned to China in the first year of Zheng-sheng (695).

It was during his second sojourn in Śrībhoja that Yijing wrote the *Record* in four fascicles sometime before 691, in which year he dispatched a Chinese monk named Dajin, whom he had met in Śrībhoja, to take the manuscript of the *Record* back to China together with his newly translated sutras and *śāstra*s in ten fascicles, and the *Biographies of Eminent Monks Who Went to the Western Regions in Search of the Dharma (Xi-yu-qiu-fa-gao-seng-zhuan)* in two fascicles, as well as a letter to the court requesting that the emperor build a Buddhist temple in India.

His motive in writing the *Record* was to provide his fellow monks at home with information about the monastic rules and manner of living of the monks in India and the islands of the South Seas. In the course of his narration and by way of comparison, Yijing did not forget to criticize the monks in China for those of their behaviors which were not in agreement with the disciplinary rules, particularly the rules of the Sarvāstivāda School. His intention was to make China a land in which Buddhism was practiced exactly as in India. In his own words he said: "My real wish is to make the Shao-shi Mountain equal to Vulture Peak, and to put the Divine Land on a par with the City of the Royal House (Rājagṛha)."

What he most objected to was the tradition of branding the scalp of a monk or nun at the time of ordination. It is said that this practice was initiated by Emperor Wu (r. 502–549) of the Liang dynasty, based on a teaching of the *Brahmajāla-sūtra* (a text on Mahayana disciplinary rules), which advocated injuring one's body by burning off a finger, cauterizing one's arms or scalp, or even committing suicide as an expression of gratitude to the Buddha. Such behavior is obviously contrary to the Vinaya rules prevalent in India. Yijing boldly deprecated these habits practiced in China and besought the monks at home to give up such improper conventions. But it seems that his admonition was not listened to, as no measures were taken to eliminate this unfortunate custom from the time that it was initiated during the first half of the sixth century C.E. until 1983, when it was abolished as a mark of ordination in all monasteries throughout China.

Again, in another chapter (Chapter Thirty-three), Yijing censured some Chinese monks for exhibiting Buddha images in the highway while performing Buddhist ceremonies in order to attract more worshipers and collect more money. This commercialization of the performance of Buddhist ceremonies was not only so popular at Yijing's time as to draw his attention but is still practiced in China without an end in view.

As a translator of Sanskrit Buddhist texts into Chinese, Yijing laid emphasis on the study of the Sanskrit language. In Chapter Thirty-four he described the principal textbooks for studying Sanskrit and remarked: "But the translators of old times rarely talked about the grammar of the Sanskrit language. . . . Now I hope you will all study Sanskrit, so that we can spare the translators the trouble of repetition. . . . Even in Ku-lun and Suli, the people can read Sanskrit scriptures. Why should the people of the Divine Land, which is a land of a bundance, not probe into the original language of the scriptures?"

It is true that Sanskrit has never been and is not a required course for Chinese student monks. Due to their lack of elementary knowledge of Sanskrit, they often misunderstood the original meaning of Chinese translations; and this gives rise to unnecessary disputes and controversies. In China there is a proverb: "Forget the trap when the fish is caught." *(De yu wang quan.)* Perhaps that was why the numerous Sanskrit texts brought back from India by Xuanzang in 645, for which a big pagoda, the Wild Goose Pagoda (Da-yan-ta), was constructed at Xi'an as a storehouse, were forgotten and not handed down to posterity.

As a source of information, Yijing's *Record* contains ample materials concerning monastic life, from the choosing of a teacher, under whose guidance one becomes a monk, up to the disposal of the personal belongings left by a deceased monk. It depicts such a complete picture of the life of a monk that it is indispensable and invaluable for research into the conditions of Buddhist monasticism in medieval India.

A RECORD OF THE INNER LAW SENT HOME FROM THE SOUTH SEAS

by

Śramaṇa Yijing

Fascicle One

Foreword

In the beginning, when the Great Chiliocosm was first produced, 204c4
it revealed the inception of the establishment of the universe. When a hundred *koṭis* (one *koṭi* equals ten million) of things were completed, there was as yet no proper order for men and inanimate objects. Since the world was hollow and empty, there was neither sun nor moon moving in it. It was really a calm and quiet state without grief or happiness, and there was no distinction between the principles of *yin* (negativity) and *yang* (positivity). Then the celestial beings of the Heaven of Purity descended, with their bodily light following them. As they took earthly delicacies, they became greedy and acquired attachment. They ate climbing plants growing in the forest and fragrant grains of rice alternately. When their bodily light gradually faded away, the sun and moon began to appear. Conjugal relations and the affairs of agriculture arose, and the relationship between ruler and the ruled as well as between father and son was established. Then the people looked up to the blue firmament above and saw that the sky was sublimely high with a colorful floating light. When they looked down to the yellow earth, they beheld that wind agitated water and solidified it into terra firma. It is said that heaven and earth were then clearly divided. Living in between were human beings who came into being spontaneously by the interaction of pure and impure vital forces. The molding and casting function of negative and positive elements was likened to a big furnace, and the production of all kinds of things was compared to the production of pottery from clay. All these were erroneous sayings due to lack of learning.

Then the mountains stood high like stars scattered about in the sky, while sentient beings spread and multiplied. They differentiated the Way into ninety-six schools and classified truth into twenty-five categories. The Sāṃkhya School holds that all things came into being from oneness, while the Vaiśeṣika School asserts that the five forms of existence arose from the six categories. Some go naked and have their hair plucked out, regarding this as the essential way of getting out of transmigration. Others smear their bodies with ashes and dress their hair into a conical topknot, clinging to this practice as a means of going up to heaven. Still others think that life is spontaneous, or that consciousness dissolves with the death of the body. Some others consider the world so obscure and profound that no one can perceive its essence, and believe that it is so subtle and incomprehensible that no one knows whence it came out. Others say that human beings will always be reborn as human beings, or say that after death they become ghosts or spirits. Some others talk about not knowing whether a butterfly becomes one's self or one's self turns into a butterfly. Some people were collectively bewildered to see a wasp which turned, when they came again, into a caterpillar. The chaos before the universe took shape was compared to an egg, and the undeveloped state of ignorance was likened to the innocent condition of an infant.

All these assertions were made due to not understanding that birth is the result of greed and present existence is the result of past actions. Will those who hold such views not transmigrate in the sea of suffering, drifting to and fro and lost in the stream of confusion?

It is our Great Teacher, the World-honored Śākyamuni, who himself pointed out a flat path, expounded the wonderful principles in person, spoke on the twelve *nidānas* (links in the chain of causality), and acquired the eighteen unique qualities of a Buddha, who is titled the Teacher of Celestial and Human Beings and the Omniscient One. He guided the four classes of living beings out of the house on fire and delivered all beings in the three realms from the city of darkness. He came out of the stream of passions and landed on the shore of nirvana (absolute extinction).

When he first attained full enlightenment at the Dragon River, 205a
all beings of the nine classes cherished the mind of renouncing this world. Then he shifted and spread the light to Deer Park, so that the living beings of the six ways fostered the mind to take refuge in him. When he first rotated the Wheel of Dharma, five persons received his edification. Next, he talked on the tradition of the disciplinary rules, and a thousand people prostrated themselves before him. Thus his pure voice was heard in the city of Rājagṛha, and those who realized the fruit of saintship were countless. In his father's city he requited him for his parental kindness, and numerous people made up their mind to acquire enlightenment. He commenced his teaching career with Ājñāta-Kauṇḍinya as his first disciple to realize the truth, and his last pupil was Subhadra in accordance with his original determination to conclude his teaching in the last period of his life. He held and maintained the Dharma for eighty years for the salvation of the beings of the nine abodes. In his teachings no obscure point was left untaught, and nobody was not accepted, however slow-witted he might be. For lay followers in general, he only spoke briefly on the five prohibitive precepts, but when speaking exclusively to the monks, he fully expounded the seven groups of the rules of discipline. It was thought that even grave offenses of householders might be absolved when the disciplinary rules were observed, and that the minor faults of the living beings might be excused when the Vinaya (moral precepts) became manifest. A monk once broke a twig with a feeling of hatred, and on account of this action he was reborn in a family of dragons. On another occasion a monk, showing mercy to small insects in the water, refused to drink it and thus was reborn in the abode of Indra after his death. The consequences of good and evil actions are as clear as that.

Thus both the sutras (scriptures) and *śāstra*s (commentaries) were taught, and mental concentration together with wisdom was employed. Isn't the Tripiṭaka (the three collections of sacred writings) the key to receiving living beings? In the presence of the Great Teacher, one always heard him preaching the same doctrine, although he taught it according to variant circumstances to save living beings. His theories vanquished other people's arguments. When he first indicated his demise at Vaiśālī, Ānanda, whose mind was deluded by Māra the Evil One, failed to ask the Great Teacher to live longer. At his last preaching near the Hiraṇyavatī River, Aniruddha revealed the truth to resolve the doubts of the audience. It may be said that this was the end of the Great Teacher's edification of living beings, and that he had completed what he could do with full merit. His physical form was no more to be seen at the two rivers, to the despair of both human and heavenly beings. His shadow faded away under the twin *śāla* trees, and even the dragons and spirits became broken-hearted. Beside the *śāla* grove the tears of the people made the ground muddy, and nearby the mourners' blood made the place look like a garden of flowering trees. With the nirvana of the Great Teacher, the world became empty and unsubstantial.

Then there were assemblies held by Dharma-propagating arhats (perfect saints), the first one being held with five hundred participants, and the second one with seven hundred participators. The keepers of the Vinaya were mainly divided into eighteen different schools, and the Tripiṭaka had variant versions according to different views and traditions. The monks of various schools wore their undergarments differently cut, either in straight lines or irregularly, and in wearing their upper robes, the folds might be made broad or narrow. When they had to lodge together, they might spend the night either in separate rooms or separated by partitions of ropes in the same room, both ways being blameless. At the time of receiving food, the monks might accept it with their hands, or mark a place on the ground to put the food on, both ways being without fault and each being handed down by a different tradition, which traditions must not be mixed together. (Yijing's running note: The Sarvāstivāda School cut the undergarments in straight lines, while the other three schools cut them

in irregular shapes. This school prescribed that monks should spend the night in separate rooms, while the Sāṃmitīya School allowed their monks to separate their beds with rope partitions. The Sarvāstivāda School permitted monks to receive food into their hands, but the Mahāsāṃghika School required them to mark a place on the ground to accept it.) The various schools and sects have different origins, and there are only four principal schools that have been handed down from the past in the Western Land. (Yijing's running note: (1) The Āryamahāsāṃghika-nikāya, or Holy School of the Great Assembly of Monks, is subdivided into seven sects, and each of the three collections of the Tripiṭaka of this school consists of a hundred thousand stanzas, which would constitute a thousand fascicles if translated into Chinese. (2) The Āryasthavira-nikāya, or School of the Holy Elders, is subdivided into three sects, and the length of its Tripiṭaka is the same as that of the preceding school. (3) The Āryamūlasarvāstivāda-nikāya, or Holy Fundamental School of Reality, is subdivided into four sects, and its Tripiṭaka is the same as that of the preceding school. (4) The Āryasāṃmitīya-nikāya, or Holy School of Correct Measures, is subdivided into four sects, and its Tripiṭaka consists
of three hundred thousand stanzas. But the subdivisions of the 205b
schools have varied according to different traditions. I have mentioned here eighteen subdivisions that exist now. As regards division into five schools, this is not heard of in the Western Land.) The schisms and their rise and fall, as well as the names of the subdivisions, are factually different, and as they are described elsewhere I need not go into detail here.

In all of the five parts of India, as well as the various islands of the South Seas, people speak of the four nikāyas, but the number of followers of the nikāyas varies at different places. In Magadha all four nikāyas are in practice, but the Sarvāstivāda-nikāya is the one most flourishing. In Lāṭa and Sindhu—names of countries in West India—three of the nikāyas have few followers, but the Sāṃmitīya has a large number of adherents. In the north all monks follow the Sarvāstivāda-nikāya, though one may sometimes meet with followers of the Mahāsāṃghika-nikāya. In the south all monks follow the Sthavira-nikāya, while the other nikāyas have few followers. In the countries at the eastern frontier, all four nikāyas are practiced in various ways. (Yijing's running note: All the places going eastward from Nālandā for five hundred post stops are known as the eastern frontier. At the extreme east there is the Great Black Mountain, which is, I reckon, the southern boundary of Tibet. It is said that it is southwest of Si-chuan, from which one may reach this mountain after a journey of a little more than a month. Further to the south from here and close to the sea coast, there is the country of Srīkṣetra. Further to the southeast is the country of Lankasu. Further to the east is the country of Dvārapati. Further to the extreme east is the country of Lin-yi. All these countries greatly venerate the triple gem. There are many men who observe the precepts, and the ascetic practice of alms-begging is the custom of the monks in these countries. In the Western Land I have seen such monks, who are really different from men of ordinary morality.)

In the Island of the Lion, all monks belong to the Sthavira-nikāya, while the Mahāsāṃghika-nikāya is repulsed. In the South Seas there are more than ten countries where only the Mūlasarvāstivāda-nikāya is predominant, though one may occasionally find some followers of the Sāṃmitīya-nikāya. Recently a few adherents of the other two nikāyas have also been found here.

(Yijing's running note: Counting from the west, there are Po-lu-si Island and then Malayu Island, which is now the country of Śrībhoja, and also Mo-he-xin Island, He-ling Island, Da-da Island, Pen-pen Island, Po-li Island, Ku-lun Island, Bhojapura Island, A-shan Island, and Mo-jia-man Island. There are also small islands, of which I cannot make a full list.) In all these countries the people follow Buddhism, but mostly of the Hinayana School, except in Malayu where there are a few Mahayana believers.

The circumference of some of these countries is about a hundred *li* (one *li* equals one-half kilometer) or several hundred *li*, or about a hundred post stations. Although it is difficult to measure the size of the great sea, those who are used to sailing in merchant ships may know it by estimation. As the people of Ku-lun were the first to come to Jiao-zhou and Guang-zhou, these places were generally called the country of Kun-lun. In this country of Kun-lun, the people have curly hair and black bodies, while the inhabitants in the other countries are not different from the people of the Divine Land of China, but they are generally barefooted and wear the *kambala* (a woolen loincloth). The details are fully described in the *Record of the South Seas*.

Traveling due south on foot from Huan-zhou for over half a month, or for five or six high tides if going on board a ship, one may reach Bi-jing, and proceeding further south one arrives at Champa, that is, Lin-yi. In this country the majority of the monks belong to the Sāṃmitīya-nikāya, with only a few adherents of the Sarvāstivāda-nikāya.

Traveling southwest for one month, one reaches the country of Banan, formerly called Funan. In old times this country was inhabited by naked people who mostly worshiped the devas. Afterwards Buddhism prevailed, but now a wicked king has completely eradicated it. No monks are found there, while various kinds of heretics live there. This is the southern seaboard of Jambudvīpa; it is not an island in the sea.

In East China, however, the main principles of Buddhism practiced are those of the Dharmagupta School, while in Central China the Mahāsāṃghika-nikāya was also followed at various places in old times. South of the Yangzi River and outside the [local] mountain range, the Sarvāstivāda-nikāya flourished in former times. We speak of the Vinaya [of the Sarvāstivāda-nikāya] as the *Vinaya of Ten Readings* and that [of the Dharmagupta-nikāya] as the *Vinaya of Four Divisions,* because these names are mainly derived from the number of sections in the Vinaya texts of these schools. Upon close observation on the distinctions between 205c
the four schools and the differences in their Vinaya texts, we see that the grave offenses and light faults are dealt with quite differently by different schools. What is permitted by one school

may be disallowed by another. The monks should observe the disciplinary rules of their respective schools, and should not substitute the rules governing light faults of other schools for those dealing with grave offenses of their own school. They should also not detest the prohibitive rules of other schools, thinking that such affairs are allowed by their own school. Otherwise the distinctions between the schools will not be apparent, and the reasons for permission and prohibition will be unclear. How can one and the same person observe the disciplinary rules of all four schools? The parable of a piece of cotton skirt and a golden staff broken into fragments indicates the realization of nirvana and that those who practice the Dharma without discrimination should behave themselves according to the rules of their respective schools. (Yijing's running note: Once King Bimbisāra dreamed that a piece of cotton cloth was torn into eighteen fragments and a golden staff broken into eighteen sections. Fearfully, he asked the Buddha about it. The Buddha said, "Over a hundred years after my nirvana, there will be a king named Aśoka ruling over Jambudvīpa. The *bhikṣus* [mendicants] will then split into eighteen schools, but the gate leading to emancipation will be one and the same for them all. Your dream is a prediction. O king, don't worry about it!")

Among the four schools there is no definite classification as to which ones should be put under Mahayana and which ones under Hinayana. In the regions of North India and the South Seas, what is prevalent is purely Hinayana, while in the Divine Land of China, the monks keep the great teaching in their minds. At other places both the Mahayana and the Hinayana are practiced in a mixed way. Through an examination of their practices, we see no differences in their disciplinary rules and restrictions. Both of them classify the Vinaya rules into five sections and practice the four noble truths. Those who worship bodhisattvas and read Mahayana scriptures are named Mahayanists, and those who do not do so are called Hinayanists. What is known as Mahayana consists of only two sub-schools, first, the Mādhyamika and second, the Yogācāra. The Mādhyamika School holds that things exist only conventionally; they are empty in reality, and their substance is void like an illusion. The Yogācāra School asserts that external phenomena do not really exist. What exists exists internally, everything being manifestations of consciousness.

Both of these two schools follow the holy teachings of the Buddha. How can we say which is right and which is wrong, since both of them lead us similarly to nirvana? And how can we say which is true and which is false, as the purpose of both schools is to cut off our passions and save all living beings? Why should we try to cause more complications and increase perplexity? If we practice according to what they teach, we shall all reach the other shore, and if we act contrary to them, we shall remain submerged in the sea of rebirth. In the Western Land, both schools are professed without having absurd contradictions in their theories, and since we have no eye of wisdom, who can judge the right and wrong of it? We should have confidence in what has long been practiced, and cultivate ourselves accordingly. We must not take the trouble to disconnect ourselves from them.

The different schools of the Vinaya observed in the Divine Land are mutually related. Lecturers and writers have produced numerous and diverse works on the Vinaya, rendering the five sections or seven groups of disciplinary rules, which had been easy to understand, difficult to comprehend. Expedient ways concerning the violation and observance of the rules had been obvious, but became obscure. Thus one's intention [to observe the Vinaya rules] dissolves at the moment when the first basketful of earth is poured down to build a mountain, and one's mind retrogresses after attending the initial lecture. Even the most talented men can achieve their learning of the Vinaya only when their mustaches have turned grey; how can men of medium or little talent gain any success even when their hair has become white? As the Vinaya texts are naturally verbose and have superfluous parts, it requires a lifetime to read all the commentaries. The established method of teachers transmitting knowledge to pupils is to discourse on chapters and sections, and explain them paragraph by paragraph and word by word; in narrating the absolution of offenses, they are analyzed sentence by sentence. To estimate the effort required for this method of study, it is as laborious as building a mountain; but so far as its advantages are concerned, it is often as lustrous as a sea pearl.

The purpose of writers is to help readers understand easily
what is written by them. How could they intentionally use inex-
206a plicit language and then try to explain away their absurdity? It is
like when a flood inundates a plain and the water vanishes into
deep wells; a thirsty man dying for want of water can by no means
save his life. But such is not the case with examination of the
Vinaya texts. For the judgment of major or minor offenses, a few
lines would be sufficient, and for explanations of the conditions
of committing faults, one need not trouble oneself for even half a
day. Such is the general tendency of the Buddhist monks of India
and the South Seas.

As regards the Divine Land, what is prevalent is the teaching of the ethical code of respecting and serving one's sovereign and parents, paying honor to and submitting to one's elders, keeping moral integrity and being modest and agreeable, and taking only what it is righteous to take. Sons should be filial to their parents and ministers loyal to the monarch. They should be prudent in conduct and lead a frugal life. The Emperor bestows great care upon his millions of subjects. As soon as the day breaks, he considers the plight of the destitute and homeless ones with pity, while none of his ministers is not respectfully executing his orders day and night with such great care as one shows when walking on thin ice. He sometimes opens a great meeting, provided with a hundred seats, to spread the teachings of the three *Yānas* (Vehicles). He has built *caityas* (temples) all over the empire, so that all men of insight turn their mind towards Buddhism, and he has also constructed *saṃghārāmas* (monasteries) throughout his domain, so that those who had gone astray turn back to the right path. The farmers sing merrily in their fields, and the merchants chant joyfully on board ship or in their carts. So the people of the countries where cocks or elephants are honored and respected come to pay homage at the red terrace in front of the Throne Hall, and the inhabitants of the regions of Golden Neighbors and Jade Ridge propose to pledge allegiance at the green moss-grown steps. Carry out things absolute; there is nothing more to be added to them. (Yijing's running note: The Cock-respecters is a name for the country of Korea used by the Indians, in whose language it is known as Kukkuṭeśvara, *kukkuṭa* meaning cock and Īśvara, respectable. It is said in India that cocks are respected as gods in Korea and that the people wear cocks' feathers by way of ornament. India is known as a country where elephants are honored because the kings of that country treat them with great honor. This is so in all five parts of India.)

As regards the homeless monks, they lecture on the disciplinary rules, with their disciples studying earnestly and respectfully learning the ultimate gists from the teachers. Some of them retire to live in a deep and secluded valley away from worldly entanglements. They wash their mouths with the water flowing down from the cliffs before they practice meditation, or sit in a jungle where they find spiritual sustenance. They practice the Way during all six periods of the day and night; by doing this they repay the kindness extended to them by those of pure faith. They go into mental concentration twice during the night; this is worthy of the respect of gods and men. Since such actions are in perfect concordance with the scriptures and the Vinaya rules, what fault can one find with them?

But errors and mistakes have crept in during the course of transmission, so that the disciplinary rules have become discrepant. Long-standing irregular forms of conduct may become regular practices which are contrary to moral principles. I have carefully written this work entitled *A Record of the Inner Law Sent Home from the South Seas* in forty chapters, divided into four fascicles, according to the holy teachings and the essential rules and regulations currently in effect. I am also sending back another book of mine, *The Memoirs of Eminent Monks Who Visited the Western*

Regions in Search of the Law during the Great Tang Dynasty, in two fascicles, together with some other miscellaneous scriptures and commentaries which I have copied. I wish that the venerable monks at home will cherish the mind of propagating the Dharma without harboring any prejudice and act with good deliberation in accordance with what the Buddha has taught, and that they will not ignore the Dharma because it is conveyed by a man of no significance.

However, the theories and concepts of the scriptures and commentaries handed down from ancient times to the present day are well interconnected with the practice of *dhyāna* (meditation). But as I am far away from you, it is difficult for me to impart to you the subtle technique of mental concentration to keep the mind in tranquility. I can, nevertheless, make a rough statement of the practices prescribed in the Vinaya texts and submit it to you in advance. The rules and regulations that I have particularized below had been checked by my teachers before I committed them to writing
206b in my *Record*. Even if I should die with the setting sun, I will still do my best to my last moment, so that when the flame of this candle goes out at dawn, a hundred lamps may continue to give light. By reading this *Record*, you may visit the five parts of India with a few steps without taking the trouble to move even one foot, and before the lapse of even a short span of time, you will be able to shed light upon the dark path for a thousand years to come. I hope that you will check and study the Tripiṭaka carefully, so as to arouse the sea of Dharma to expunge the four grievous offenses, and that with the five sections of the Vinaya rules, which are as clear as a mirror, you will sail the boat of wisdom to save those who are submerged in the river of six desires. Although I have received personal instructions from my teachers and what I have learned does not arise from my own originality, I am afraid that I may in the end be sneered at by men endowed with the eye of wisdom. This is all I have to say.

All the topics discussed here are discussed according to the Mūlasarvāstivāda School; the traditions of other schools should

not be intermingled with discussions of this work. The matters mentioned here are generally the same as those related in the *Daśasvādhyāya-vinaya* (the *Vinaya of Ten Readings*) of the Sarvāstivāda School, which has three sub-sects, namely, (1) the 206c
Dharmagupta, (2) the Mahīśāsaka, and (3) the Kāśyapīya. These sub-sects are not prevalent in the five parts of India, except in Udyāna, Kucha, and Kustana, where there are some adherents of these sub-sects mixed with the followers of other schools. Yet the *Daśasvādhyāya-vinaya* does not belong to the Mūlasarvāstivāda School.

A Record of the Inner Law Sent Home from the South Seas

1. No Degradation Is Caused by a Breach of the Summer Retreat

Those *bhikṣus* who have broken away from the summer retreat are merely disqualified from receiving the ten benefits therefrom; it is unjustifiable to degrade them from their original position of seniority in the community of monks. How is it tolerable that a monk who used to receive homage from others at former times should now pay respect in reverse order to his juniors? Habitual forms of conduct like this may become customary but are groundless practices. The acceptance of a special invitation to a monk to go out during the summer retreat is as serious an offense as to earn a living by theft. Therefore, we should make a careful examination of this matter and must not neglect it. The priority of a monk's position should be determined by the date of his ordination. Even if he should fail to observe the summer retreat properly, he must not be degraded in position, because no such prescription is found in the holy teachings. Who was the person that at some former time initiated this practice?

2. Behavior towards the Honored Ones

According to the teachings of the Buddha, it is decorous for a monk to go barefoot in the presence of a holy statue or upon approaching his honored teachers, except if he is ill; wearing shoes or other footgear is not allowed under such circumstances. He must keep his right shoulder bare and cover his left arm with his robe, without wearing a kerchief or a turban. Such is the regular way, but he may be allowed to do otherwise without committing any fault when he is walking in other places. If he is in a cold country, he is permitted to put on short boots or shoes suitable to the local climate. As the climate may be hot or cold in different places and regions, many of the rules are adaptable according to the holy teachings. It is reasonable that a monk is allowed to wear warm clothes temporarily during the months of severe winter to keep the body in good health. But during the spring and summer seasons, a monk must act according to the regulations of the Vinaya. One should not circumambulate a Buddha's tope while wearing shoes; this was clearly taught at the very beginning. Those who wear laced boots must not enter temples; this has been declared long ago. But there are people who willfully violate this rule. They are rudely disregarding the golden words.

3. Sitting on Small Chairs at Mealtimes

The monks of India in the west must wash their hands and feet before taking meals, and they each sit on a small chair which is about seven inches high and only a foot square. The seat, being woven out of rattan cane and having round legs, is light to carry. For junior or younger monks, small pieces of wood the size of a chopping block may serve as seats. They place their feet on the ground, and plates and jars are put in front of them. The ground is smeared with cow's dung by way of purification, with fresh leaves spread over it. The chairs are arranged at intervals of one cubit, so that the monks sitting on them do not touch each other.

I have never seen monks [in India] sitting cross-legged on big couches to take meals. According to the holy regulations, the length of a couch measures eight fingers of the Buddha. As the Buddha's fingers are three times longer than those of an ordinary man, the length of a couch comes to twenty-four fingers of an ordinary man, corresponding to one and a half times the Chinese *hu* ruler (a ceremonial tablet used by officials at court). In the monasteries of
207a China in the east, the height of a couch exceeds two feet, but such

a couch was originally unfit for a monk to sit on, as it is an offense for a monk to sit on a high couch. At present, many monks do sit on high couches, and what can we do about it? Those who incur blame should make a study of the prescribed measurement of couches. But in the Ling-yan and Si-chan Monasteries, the couches they use are one foot high. There was a reason for the virtuous people of ancient times to make this rule. One should know that sitting cross-legged side by side with knees put in a line is not the right manner for monks to take meals.

I have heard that in the beginning, when Buddhism was introduced into China, all monks sat squatting on their heels at mealtimes. This was so up to the Jin dynasty (265–419), when this manner of sitting to take meals came to be considered erroneous. Since then the monks have sat cross-legged to take meals. Seven hundred years have passed since the holy teachings spread to China in the east. Ten dynasties have gone by through this period, and each dynasty had its own prominent monks. Indian monks visited China one after another, and Chinese monks lined up to receive instruction from them. Some Chinese monks also went personally to India in the west and witnessed what was right and what was wrong. When they returned home, they told their fellow monks what they had seen abroad, but who would listen to them?

It is said in a scripture, "After taking food, they washed their feet." It is clear that the monks were not sitting cross-legged on couches to take their meal; they washed their feet because food remnants were dropped on the ground near their feet. From this we may know that the monks sat with their feet on the ground while eating. Disciples of the Buddha should follow the example of the Buddha. Even if it is hard for them to keep the rules, they must not deride them.

If a monk spreads a kerchief and sits on it with his legs crossed squarely, it is difficult for him to keep himself clean, as it is impossible to avoid getting stained in this posture by food remnants and spills. Moreover, to collect what has been left over from a meal does not at all conform with Indian custom. To collect the leftovers would pollute the plates used by the monks; the servants touch only clean and pure tableware. This is an inane tradition which is ineffective for the preservation of purity. Please make a good examination of these points and see what are the merits and demerits.

4. The Distinction between Pure and Impure Food

It is customary for both monks and laypeople of India in the west to differentiate between clean and unclean food. If only a mouthful of food has been eaten, it all becomes defiled, and even the receptacle is unfit for reuse and must be put aside to be discarded together with other used containers after the meal is over. All leftover food is given to those who are suited to eat it. To collect and preserve it for further use is never allowed. All people of high or low rank keep this custom, which is a convention observed not only by men but also by deities.

Therefore, it is said in several commentaries: "It is considered disdainful not to chew a willow twig [to cleanse the teeth], not to wash one's self after defecation, and not to distinguish between pure and impure food." How can we use defiled utensils to convey food once again, collect and preserve leftovers in the kitchen, put surplus cooked rice back in the pot, return the remaining soup to the thermal vessel, eat the next morning what broth and vegetables are left overnight, and keep cakes and fruits to be eaten the day after tomorrow? Those who observe the Vinaya rules know well about this distinction, but those who are undisciplined make no distinction between them and regard them as identical.

On the occasion of receiving offerings of food, or at other times when an ordinary meal is taken, a monk is considered defiled as soon as he has put food into his mouth, and he must not touch others, nor take another dish of clean food, unless he has rinsed

his mouth with pure water. If he touches another person before washing his mouth, the person he has touched becomes defiled 207b
too, and that person must wash himself. If he has touched a dog, he must also wash himself.

When offering sacrificial food to deities, the person who performs the rites should stand to one side. After the ceremony is over, he should wash his hands and rinse his mouth, and also wash the sacrificial utensils. Then he may touch the cooking pans and pots. Otherwise his supplication and incantation will be inefficacious, and even if sacrificial food is offered, the deities will not accept it. Therefore, we may say that whatever offerings are prepared either for presenting to the triple gem, or for giving to the spirits, or even for ordinary meals, must be pure and clean. If a monk has not washed himself clean and rinsed his mouth, and has not washed after relieving nature, he is unfit to prepare food. As the common saying goes: "Only pure food may be offered as a sacrifice to the deceased. Nails must be clipped cleanly right to the flesh [when making such an offering]. Whether it is for those who have abandoned this mundane world, or for such people as Confucius and his disciple Yan Hui, food offered as a sacrifice must be pure and clean, and leftovers are never used as offerings to the deceased." For the preparation of food as an offering, or as a regular meal for the monks, a superintendent is needed to oversee the process. While waiting for the preparation, if a monk or a layman fears that he might be delayed beyond the prescribed time for taking a meal, he may take a portion of food and eat it separately before the meal is properly served. This is permitted by the teachings of the Buddha and it is faultless.

I have recently seen that under the supervision of monks and nuns, meals are often served after noontime. In this way they committed a fault instead of gaining bliss; one must not do so. The fundamental difference between the five parts of India and other countries is this distinction between purity and impurity. Once some messengers of the Hu tribe in the north [of China] came to India in the west, and they were laughed at by the local people, because they did not wash themselves after answering the call of nature, kept leftovers in a pot, sat so closely together as to touch each other at mealtimes, did not keep back from pigs and dogs, and did not chew willow twigs to cleanse their teeth. Thus they incurred ridicule and censure. Therefore, Dharma practitioners should be extremely mindful of these matters and must not think of them as trivialities. But in China no distinction was ever made between pure and impure food since the remote past. Although the monks have heard about it, they never have put the rules into practice, and until I speak to them in person, they will not get a real understanding of it.

5. Cleansing after Taking Meals

After having taken a meal, a monk must wash his hands, then clean and chew a willow twig to cleanse, brush, and pick his teeth, as well as scrape his tongue, so as to make them all clean. He may do so either with a vessel to contain the used water, or at some secluded place, or over the opening of a drain, or near the flight of steps leading to a house. He may hold the water jar himself, or ask someone to provide water for him. If saliva remains in his mouth, he is considered not to have observed the fast. After that, he should use bean dregs, or sometimes mud made of earth mixed with water, to wipe his lips to clear away the smell of grease. After that, he should pour the water from a clean jar into a conch-shell cup, which is placed either on a piece of fresh leaf or in the hand. Both the vessel and the hand must be cleaned with three kinds of dregs, i.e., bean dregs, dry earth, and cow's dung, in order to wash away the grease. Or he may pour the water from a clean jar into his mouth at some secluded place, but if he is at an open
207c place, he is forbidden to do so by the Vinaya rules. Just gargle two or three times; the mouth will be washed clean. Before doing so a monk is not allowed to swallow saliva, as it is not only a breach of etiquette but also a faulty behavior. Before the mouth has been

rinsed again with pure water, the saliva must be spat out. If he did not do so after noontime, he would be considered to have violated the rule not to eat at irregular times. People seldom know about this point, and even if they know this rule, it is not easy for them to keep it. From this point of view, we may say that even the use of bean dregs or ash water can hardly keep us entirely free from fault, as food particles may still remain between the teeth and grease still stick on the tongue.

The wise ones should see into and be mindful about these points. It is not allowed for a monk to pass his time gossiping and talking after the meal is properly over, nor is he permitted not to keep a jar full of pure water and not to chew the tooth-cleaning twig, having an unclean mouth for the whole morning and incurring blame throughout the night. If one lives in this way till the end of life, it would be a disaster indeed! To ask a disciple to hold the jar and pour out the pure water for washing is also in conformity with the rules.

6. Two Bottles for Keeping Water

Water is used differently for pure and impure purposes, and it is kept separately in two bottles. Earthenware or porcelain bottles are used for keeping water for pure purposes, and copper or iron ones, for impure purposes. The pure water is kept for drinking in the afternoon, while the impure water is needed for washing after going to the latrine. The pure water bottle must be held with the clean hand and be stored in a clean place, and the bottle containing water for impure purposes should be grasped with the unclean hand and be put away at some unclean place. Only the water contained in a clean bottle, or in some new and clean vessel, is fit for drinking in the afternoon, while the water contained in other vessels is called "timely water," which can be drunk without fault at noontime or before noon, but it is faulty to drink it in the afternoon.

In making a water bottle, there must be a lid to cover the outlet, which is about two finger-widths high, and on the top is a small hole, of a size that would allow a copper chopstick to be put in. One may drink the water from this spout. At the side of the bottle, there is another round holc as large as a coin with a mouth projecting two finger-widths high. The bottle is replenished through this hole. It may contain two or three liters of water. Bottles of smaller size are not used. If one fears that insects and dust may enter the bottle through these two apertures, one may cover them up, or close them with stoppers made of bamboo, wood, linen, or leaves.

The Indian monks make their water bottles after this fashion. At the time of taking water, the inside of the bottle must be washed clean and free of any dust or filth before taking in fresh water. How can we take water without regarding whether it is pure or not, simply keeping it in a small copper jug and pouring it out with the lid covering the mouth, so that the water spills and splashes? It is [then] unfit for use, because it is hard to know whether the water kept in [the jug] is pure or not, as it may be dirty and smelly inside, not suitable for keeping water at all. Moreover, the amount—one liter and two deciliters—of water contained in it is not sufficient for doing anything.

For making a bag for the bottle, a piece of cloth about two feet long and one foot wide may be used. Fold the cloth to make the two ends meet and sew the edges together. Strings about the length of one span are attached to the upper corners for fastening the opening of the bag. The bag is hung on the monk's shoulder with a bottle inside it. When a monk is going round begging for food, the
208a bag for his alms bowl is also made in the same fashion. It should cover the mouth of the bowl to keep dust from entering it. As the bottom of the bag is made in a pointed shape, the bowl does not turn about in it. But the bag for storing the bowl is different from that for the bottle, as is described elsewhere. When a monk is traveling, he carries his bottle, alms bowl, personal robes, and other articles separately on his shoulders, and, fully covered with his

kāṣāya (religious robe), he goes away with an umbrella in his hand. These are the manners of Buddhist monks.

If he has a free hand, he may carry a bottle for unclean purposes and a bag containing his leather shoes, and hold a staff with tin rings obliquely under his arm, while proceeding or stopping on the way composedly, just as is described in the *Sutra on the Parable of the Crow and the Moon*.

At the season of worshiping the *caitya*s, monks flocked from the four quarters to Rājagṛha, the bodhi tree, Vulture Peak, Deer Park, the place of the *śāla* trees which once burst into bloom with white blossoms resembling a flock of cranes, and the desolate Kukkuṭapāda Mountain. Every day I saw thousands of monks attired in the above-mentioned style. As regards the learned monks of great virtue of Nālandā Monastery, they rode in palanquins, but never on horseback, and the monks of Mahārāja Monastery did the same. All their requisite articles were carried for them by other persons or by grooms. Such is the rule of the monks of India in the west.

7. Morning Inspection of Water to Clear Away Insects

Water must be inspected every morning. As water comes from different sources, from a bottle, a well, a pond, or a river, it is not inspected according to one uniform standard. At dawn, bottle water is first examined by pouring out a handful of it from a clean white copper cup, a copper dish, a conch-shell cup, or a lacquer vessel, onto a piece of brick. A wooden instrument may also be made for the special purpose of examining water. With one's mouth covered by one's hand, one should observe the water for a good while. One may also observe the water in a basin or a pot. Even insects as tiny as a hair-point must be treated mindfully. If any insect has been found, the water should be returned to the bottle, which should be washed again and again until no insect is left in it.

If there is a pond or a river, take the bottle there and pour the water with the insects into it, and then refill the bottle with filtered fresh water. If there is only a well, strain the water in the usual way. In examining the water of a well, one should first draw some water from the well, get a cupful of it from the pail with a copper cup, and then examine it as stated above. If there is no insect in it, the water can be used throughout the night, and if there is any insect, strain the water as mentioned before. As regards the inspection of water of a pond or a river, it is explained in detail in the Vinaya.

For the filtration of water, the Indians in the west use the best white kapok cloth, but in China fine silk may be used. The silk should be starched with rice gruel or slightly boiled in water. Take a piece of boiled silk, four *hu* feet long. Hold the edges to pull it sidewards, and then put the two ends together and sew them up into the shape of a sieve. Laces are attached to the two corners, and loops to both sides. A stick is put across the silk in the middle to stretch it to one foot and six inches wide. The two ends of the strainer are fastened to posts and a basin is placed under it. When water is poured into it from a pot, the bottom of the pot must be
208b inside the strainer. Otherwise the insects might drop with the water to the ground, or into the basin, where they would be bound to be killed. When water has just been poured into the strainer, hold it and see. If there is any insect, the strainer should be changed. If it is clean as usual, it may be used again. When sufficient water has been poured into it, the strainer may be turned inside out. Two persons, each holding one end, turn out the strainer into a life-preserving vessel, pour water over it three times, and then rinse it from outside. Water is put into it once again to make another examination. If no insect is found, the strainer may be stored away at will.

When this [filtered] water has been kept overnight, it must be reexamined. It is said in the Vinaya that the use of the water that has been kept overnight without being reexamined in the morning incurs guilt, whether it does or does not have insects.

There are many different ways of protecting life while drawing water. The strainer mentioned above is adequate for use at a well. At a river or a pond, one may fix a wooden bowl and use a double bottle as a temporary makeshift for a strainer. During the sixth and seventh months of the year, the insects are smaller and different from what they are at other times, and they can penetrate ten layers of raw silk. Those who rejoice in protecting life should be mindful to spare them. An earthenware basin may be made for the purpose, but the silk strainer is useful and simple to make. In the monasteries of India in the west, the basin is mostly made of copper. As this is also done in accordance with the rules laid down by the Buddha, one must not disdain it.

The life-preserving vessel is a small water pot with an open mouth as big as the pot itself. There are two noses at the sides near the bottom, and strings are fastened to them. When it has been put into the water, pull the strings to turn it upside down and plunge it into the water over and over again before it is pulled out.

If a strainer is for common use in a monastery, it is unbefitting on principle for a fully ordained monk to touch it, nor should he take the "timely water" kept in his chamber. He may drink it only when it is brought to him by a monk not fully ordained. When drinking water at irregular times, one must use a pure strainer, a pure bottle, and a pure cup, and then one may drink it. The preservation of life is a disciplinary rule pertaining to natural morality. Among the rules of prohibition, taking life is a major violation, and it is at the head of the ten evil deeds. This should by no means be ignored or slighted.

The strainer, being one of the six requisites of a monk, is an indispensable article for him to possess. Without a strainer, one should not travel even for three or five *li*. If a monk is aware that strainers are not used in a monastery, it is unbefitting for him to partake of a meal there. One would rather die of thirst [than drink unfiltered water] on a long journey, and this is sufficient to be a good example for us. How can we use our daily water without inspecting it?

Although some monks do use strainers, they let the insects die inside them. Even if they intend to save life, they seldom know the rules for doing it. They overturn the strainers over the mouth of a well, not knowing to use a life-preserver. Once the insects reach the water in the well, they are killed without doubt. Sometimes the monks make a small, round strainer out of raw, rough, and thin silk, capable of receiving only twelve deciliters of water. They do not look for insects in the strainer, but simply hang it up beside their alms bowl to let people see and know that it is there. They have no mind to protect life, and they commit faults everyday. They act in this manner, which is handed down from teacher to disciple, thinking that they are transmitting the Dharma! What a pity, and how regretful it is indeed! Everybody should keep his own vessel for inspection of water, and life-preservers should be provided at all places.

8. Chewing Tooth Wood in the Morning

208c Every day in the morning, a monk must chew a piece of tooth wood to brush his teeth and scrape his tongue, and this must be done in the proper way. Only after one has washed one's hands and mouth may one make salutations. Otherwise both the saluter and the saluted are at fault. In Sanskrit the tooth wood is known as the *dantakāṣṭha*—*danta* meaning tooth, and *kāṣṭha*, a piece of wood. It is twelve finger-widths in length. The shortest is not less than eight finger-widths long, resembling the little finger in size. Chew one end of the wood well for a long while and then brush the teeth with it. If one has to go near a superior person [while chewing a tooth wood], one should cover the mouth with the left hand. After having used the wood for brushing the teeth, split and bend it to scrape the tongue. One may also use copper or iron to make a tongue-scraper. A thin flat piece of bamboo or wood, the size of the surface of the little finger and sharpened at one end, may be used as a toothpick to clean broken teeth. When the wood is bent to scrape the tongue, take care not to hurt it. After having been used, the wood may be washed clean and discarded in some secluded place. When discarding the tooth wood, or spitting out water or saliva, one must snap one's fingers three times, or cough more than twice. Otherwise it would be a fault to discard them. Or one may break up a large piece of wood or cut a slender branch into short pieces to make tooth wood. Near a mountain or a village, one should give priority to the use of the branches of quercus, bine, and ampelopsis, while on the plains, one may collect in advance branches of mulberry, peach, locust tree, and willow at will, and keep them in store, so that they will not run short. Fresh twigs should be offered to others, while dry ones may be retained for one's own use. The younger monks may take the twigs and chew them at will, but the elders have to strike one end of the twig with a hammer to make it soft.

Twigs of a bitter, astringent, or pungent taste, the end of which may become cotton-like after being chewed, are best for using as tooth wood. The rough root of burweed is the most excellent for this purpose. (Yijing's running note: That is the root of xanthium. Cut its root two inches under the ground.) It hardens the teeth and makes the mouth good-smelling, and also helps the digestion and cures heart disease. After using this root for half a month, foul breath will disappear, and toothache or dental disease can be healed after thirty days. One must chew the tooth wood well and wipe one's teeth clean. Let all the saliva and oozing blood come out of the mouth, and then rinse it clean with a large quantity of water. Such is the way of cleansing the mouth.

After that, if one can take in a spoonful of water through the nose, that would be practicing Nāgārjuna's art of longevity. If one is not accustomed to taking in water through one's nose, to drink water is also good. When this method is used for a long time, one will get less sickness. Dental calculus accumulates at the root of the teeth and is hardened through the passage of time; it should be completely scraped off. When the mouth is gargled clean, the teeth will not decay any more till the end of one's life. Toothache is almost unknown in India because the people there chew tooth wood.

We must not mistake the tooth wood for willow twigs. In the whole country of India, the willow is scarcely seen. Although the translators used this name, the wood for the Buddha's tooth wood was not actually from the willow tree. I have seen it with my own
209a eyes at Nālandā Monastery. I am not trying to convince others about this matter, but my readers need not take the trouble to doubt it. Even in the Sanskrit text of the *Nirvana Sutra*, there is the saying: "At the time of chewing tooth wood. . . ."

Some monks [in China] use five or six small willow twigs and chew them all in their mouths, not knowing how to rinse out the dregs. Some of them swallow the juice, thinking that it will cure their ailments. They try to be clean, but contrarily they become filthy, and though they hope to get rid of disease, they incur more serious illness. They may be unaware of this fact, and they are out of the limits of our discussion. According to the custom of the five parts of India, tooth wood is regularly chewed, and even a child of three is taught how to do it. Both the holy teachings of the Buddha and the secular custom of the people advocate this beneficial habit. I have explained the meritorious and demeritorious ways of chewing tooth wood, and it is up to my reader to decide at his own discretion whether he should practice or reject this custom.

9. Acceptance of an Invitation to a Feast

Concerning how monks go to attend a feast in India and the other countries of the South Seas, I shall give a brief description of the ceremony.

In India, the donor comes beforehand to the monks, and after paying homage to them, he invites them to attend the feast. On the festival day, he comes to inform them, "It is time [for the feast]." Utensils and seats for the monks are prepared according to circumstances. They may either use their own vessels, carried by monastic servants for them, or use the clean articles provided by the donor. The utensils are made solely of copper, which must be rubbed clean with fine ashes. Each monk sits in a small chair, placed at such a distance that one person does not touch another. The structure of the chairs has already been described in Chapter Three.

Earthenware vessels that have not been used before may be used only once without fault. Once they have been used, they are thrown away into a pit or ditch, because defiled vessels should not be collected for further use. That is why in the western country of India, huge heaps of used vessels are piled up high at places beside the road where alms of food have been given, and none of them is to be used again. But earthenware of good quality, such as that produced at Xiangyang, may be collected after having been used, as once they are discarded they may be washed clean by way of purification. In the five parts of India, there were formerly no porcelain and lacquer works. Porcelain vessels, which look as if made of clay mixed with oil, are clean without doubt. Lacquer articles are sometimes brought to India by merchants, but the people of the South Seas never use them as eating vessels because such articles are liable to become greasy. But if the vessels are new ones, they may be used as well after the smell of grease is cleansed away with pure ashes. Wooden vessels are not used for tableware. However, new ones may be used once without it being considered a fault, but it is an error to use them a second time. This matter is related in the Vinaya.

In the donor's house, the ground must be smeared with cow's dung at the place where the feast is prepared, and small chairs are arranged separately one by one. A large quantity of water is stored in clean jars in advance. When the monks arrive at the house, they untie the fastenings of their robes. After examining the water in the clean jars prepared for them, they wash their feet with it, if no insect has been found in it. Then they take their seats in the small chairs and rest for a while. Having observed the time and finding that the sun is nearly at the zenith, the donor

makes the announcement that the time has arrived [for partaking of the feast]. Then each of the monks folds his upper robe and ties the two corners up in front, while taking up the right corner of the lower side and pressing it under the girdle at his left side.
209b The monks wash their hands clean with bean powder or earth, either with the donor pouring water for them, or with the monks themselves using water from the *kuṇḍikā* (jars). This is done according to which way is more convenient. Then they return to their seats and receive the eating vessels, which they wash slightly without letting the water overflow. Before taking the meal, they never say prayers. Having washed his hands and feet, the donor places food as a sacrificial offering to the holy monks at the beginning of the row of seats, and then distributes food to the monks one by one. At the end of the row, a plate of food is placed as an offering to Mother Hāritī.

Once in her former life, this mother made a vow for some reason or other to devour all the babies in Rājagṛha. Owing to her wicked vow, she forfeited her life and was reborn as a *yakṣī* (female demon). She gave birth to five hundred children and ate some male or female babies of Rājagṛha every day. The people told this to the Buddha, who, therefore, concealed her little son, named Beloved Son. In the course of seeking her lost son in many places, the *yakṣī* at last found her child where the Buddha was. The World-honored One said to her, "Are you sorry for the loss of your Beloved Son? You grieved at the loss of only one out of your five hundred children, yet how much more pained are those who had only one or two children and have lost them?" Then the Buddha converted the *yakṣī* and made her observe the five precepts as an *upāsikā* (female devotee).

The *yakṣī* asked the Buddha, "I have five hundred children. What shall we eat hereafter?" The Buddha said in reply, "In the monasteries where the *bhikṣus* dwell, they will make daily offerings of food as meals for you and yours to eat." For this reason, in the monasteries of India in the west, images or portraits of Hāritī, depicting her holding a baby in her arms, with three or five children round her knees, are found on the porch or in a corner in the kitchen. Every day abundant offerings of food are placed before this image. Being a subject of the four heavenly kings, this mother has the power to enrich people. If those who are suffering from illness or are childless offer sacrificial food to her, their wish will always be fulfilled. A full account of her is given in the Vinaya; I have just related the story in brief. In the Divine Land of China, she was formerly known as the Mother of Demoniac Children.

Moreover, in the great monasteries of India, a wooden statue of a deity, two or three feet high, is placed beside a pillar in the kitchen or in front of the gate of the main storehouse. The deity is seated in a small chair with a golden bag in his hand and one foot hanging down to the ground. Black in color and often anointed with oil, he is called Mahākāla, or the Great Black Deity. Ancient tradition says that he is a subordinate of Maheśvara. By nature he adores the triple gem and extends protection to the five groups of Buddhist clergy, so that they will not sustain any damage. Those who say prayers to him have their wishes fulfilled. At mealtimes, the cooks always offer incense and lamps to the deity and place before him all kinds of food and drink.

Once I saw more than a hundred resident monks having their meal at Bandhana Monastery, the site where the Buddha preached the *Mahāparinirvāṇa-sūtra*. In the spring and autumn seasons worshipers would arrive unexpectedly. One day five hundred monks suddenly came at about midday, and as it was exactly noontime, it was inconvenient for the resident monks to prepare more food for the uninvited guests. The managing monk said to the cooks, 209c
"In such a hurry, what can we do?" Then an old woman, the mother of a monastic servant, told him, "This is a normal affair, don't worry about it." She burned much incense, lit many lamps, and offered abundant sacrificial food to the Black Deity, to whom she said, "Although the Great Sage has entered nirvana, divine beings like you still exist. Now monks of the four quarters have come to worship this holy site. Let not the offerings of food and drink be deficient for them. You have the power to do this, and you know this is the time."

Then all the monks were invited to take seats, and the regular amount of food for the resident monks of the monastery was served to them all one by one. Every one of the great assembly of monks was fully satisfied, while the leftover food was just as much as usual. All of them shouted, *"Sādhu, sādhu!"* ("Excellent, excellent!"), and praised the power of the deity. I went there in person to worship the holy site. Thus I saw the features of that deity, before whom enormous heaps of food were placed as offerings. When I asked the reason, the monks told me the above story. Images of this deity were not formerly found in the areas north of the Huai River in China; however, they were installed in many monasteries south of the Yangzi River. Suppliants who prayed to the deity always got favorable responses, and his spiritual efficacy was not illusory. The *nāga* Mahāmucilinda of Mahābodhi Monastery also has such miraculous powers.

Food is served to the monks in the following way. First, one or two pieces of ginger about the size of a thumb and one or half a spoonful of salt placed on a leaf are distributed to each of the monks. The person who serves the salt folds his hands palm to palm and kneels before the chief monk while chanting, *"Saṃprāgatam,"* meaning "well come." The old transliteration *sam-ba* is erroneous. Then the chief monk says in reply, "Serve the food equally."

The utterance of the [Sanskrit] word is to indicate that the meal has been well prepared and it is time to serve the food. It should be understood as such according to the meaning of the word. Once the Buddha and his group of disciples received poisoned food from someone, and he taught them to say *"Saṃprāgatam."* When they took the meal, all the poison turned to delicious food. From this incident we may say that this word is also a mystic formula, not merely meaning "well come." This word may be pronounced either in the eastern (Chinese) or in the western (Indian) way, as one wishes, at the time of uttering it. In the districts of Bing and Fen, the monks chant it *shi zhi* (the time has arrived), and they have a good reason for it.

The person who serves the food must stand respectfully, with his two feet close together, and bow before the recipient of the food. He holds a vessel with cakes and fruits in his hands. The edibles should be dropped into the hand of the diner from one span above it, while other kinds of food are put into the diner's vessel from one or two inches above it. Otherwise acceptance is not in conformity with the rules concerning a monk taking things from others. A monk may begin to eat as soon as his share of food is distributed to him; he need not wait till food is served to all the partakers of the meal. To wait for food to be served to all monks is not a correct interpretation of good demeanor. Nor is it in agreement with the holy teaching to act as one wishes after a meal is over.

Next, cooked round-grained nonglutinous rice, together with thick bean soup, is served with hot ghee. The monks mix the rice and soup with their fingers, and add various condiments to the mixed food, which they eat with their right hands. When one is just half satiated with the food, cakes and fruits are served, and after that yogurt is served with granulated sugar. When the monks are thirsty, they drink cold water, whether it is winter or sum- 210a
mer. This is a brief account of how the monks take their daily meal or attend a reception.

For making an offering of food to the monks, it is customary to show hospitality by preparing a large amount of edibles, so much that plates and bowls brim over with leftover cakes and rice, while as much ghee and yogurt may be consumed as one wishes. In the Buddha's time, King Prasenajit once personally offered food to the Buddha and his assembly of disciples. So much food, drink, ghee, and yogurt were prepared to serve them that the victuals overflowed on the ground. This event is mentioned in the Vinaya.

When I first arrived in the country of Tāmralipti in East India, I intended to prepare a plain and moderate meal as an offering to entertain the monks. Someone advised me not to do so, saying, "You can, of course, prepare just enough food for a feast; but according to ancient tradition, one must make it a rich and sumptuous affair. If the food is just enough to fill the stomach, I am afraid people will laugh at you. I have heard that you come from a great country where everything is abundant. If you cannot afford the expense, you had better not prepare the feast." Thus I acted according to their custom, which is not unreasonable, because the mind of giving generous alms will get a rich reward. But a poor man may present whatever gifts he can afford to the monks after a meal is over.

When the meal is over, the monks wash their mouths with a little water, which is swallowed instead of being spat out. Some water is put into a basin, in which a monk may wash his right hand briefly, and after that he may stand up from his seat. When he is about to stand up, he should take a handful of food in his right hand, whether it is food offered to the Buddha or distributed to the monks, to be taken out and given as alms to all living beings in accordance with the holy teaching. But it is not taught in the Vinaya to give away food before the meal. A plateful of food is also taken out as an offering to the dead and other deities and spirits, as well as to those who are worthy of eating it. This custom has its origin at Vulture Peak, as is related in detail in a scripture. One may bring the food to the chief monk and kneel before him. The chief monk then sprinkles a few drops of water on the food and utters the following prayer:

> May what blessedness we have cultivated
> Benefit universally those in the realm of ghosts.
> After eating the food, they may escape from their plight
> And be reborn after death in a blissful site.
> The happiness a bodhisattva enjoys
> Is as limitless as empty space.
> By alms-giving one may get such fruits,
> Which will augment without cease.

Then the food is taken out and placed in a quiet spot or under a tree, or thrown into a river or a pond, as alms given to the deceased. In the regions between the Yangzi and the Huai Rivers in China, the people prepare a separate plateful of food besides the meal offered to the monks. This is the custom described above.

After the meal is over, the donor gives tooth wood and pure water to the monks. How to wash one's hands and mouth has been related in Chapter Five. At the time of taking leave of the donor, the monks say to him, “We rejoice at whatever meritorious deeds you have done!” And then they disperse.

There is no other religious ceremony [performed in connection with the feast], except that each of the monks recites a stanza by himself. As for the leftovers after a meal, the monks are at liberty to order a boy to carry it away, or to give it to poor and low people or any others who need the food to eat. Or if it happens to be a 210b
year of famine, or if they fear that the donor might be of a stingy nature, they should ask for his permission before taking away the leftover food. But the donor of the feast should by no means collect the remains of the meal for himself. Such is the way that monks receive offerings of food in India.

Or the donor may invite monks to his house as described before. He should set up an image of the Buddha at his house beforehand. When noontime is approaching, the monks go to the holy image and crouch down with their hands joined palm to palm to venerate the Buddha’s memory. After paying homage to the Buddha’s image, they eat in the manner related before. Or they may ask someone from among themselves to go and kneel erect before the holy image with his hands joined palm to palm and praise the Buddha in a loud voice. (Yijing’s running note: This erect kneeling means both knees touch the ground while the thighs support the body erect. In old times it was known as kneeling in the way of the Hu people. But it is wrong to say so, because the erect kneeling is popular in all five parts of India, so how can it be said to be the kneeling of the Hu people alone?) The monk who is asked to praise the Buddha only sings of the Buddha’s virtues; nothing else is said.

Then the donor lights lamps, scatters flowers with single-minded devotion, rubs the monks’ feet with perfumed paste, and burns incense in profusion. All this is not usually done by different persons. Meanwhile, according to circumstances, drums and stringed instruments may be played to accompany songs as an offering of music. Then the meal is served to each of the monks one by one as has been described before. When the meal is over, water is provided from a bottle in front of the monks. After that the chief monk utters a short *dānagāthā* (a verse to express gratitude) to the donor. Such is another way that monks receive offerings of food in India.

Although the manner of eating in the western country of India is different in many ways from that of China, I will make a brief account of the Indian way of eating according to the rules of the Vinaya.

In the Vinaya the Sanskrit terms *pañcabhojanīya* and *pañcakhādanīya* are mentioned. The word *bhojanīya* means regular food, and *khādanīya*, what is chewed and eaten. As *pañca* means five, *pañcabhojanīya* should be translated into Chinese as five kinds of edibles, which were formerly known as the five kinds of regular food according to the semantic meaning of the word. They are (1) cooked rice, (2) mixed meal made of barley and beans, (3) parched rice flour, (4) meat, and (5) cakes. The word *pañcakhādanīya* should be translated as the five kinds of masticated food, namely, (1) roots, (2) stalks, (3) leaves, (4) flowers, and (5) fruits. If one has no choice but to eat the first group of food, one would certainly not like to eat anything of the second group, but if one has first eaten food of the second category, one might still wish to eat some more of the first category. We know that milk, yogurt, etc., are not included in the two groups of food, because no such names are separately mentioned in the Vinaya, and it is clear that they do not belong to the class of regular food. Any food made of wheat flour, if so solid that a spoon put into it stands erect without slanting any way, is included under cakes and cooked rice. Dry rice flour mixed with water is also included under one of the five kinds of [regular] food, if it is so thick that finger traces remain visible on its surface.

The boundaries of the five parts of India are extensive and remote, and, roughly speaking, the length of the radius stretching to the four quarters of the land is more than four hundred post stations. Although I did not see all things with my own eyes at places other than the frontier regions, I could make careful inquiries

to find out about them. All edibles, whether for eating or chewing, are exquisitely prepared in different ways. In the north, wheat flour is plentiful, while in the west, baked rice flour is abundant. In the country of Magadha, wheat flour is scarce, but rice is abundant. The southern frontier and the eastern borderland grow the same crops as Magadha. Ghee and yogurt are found everywhere, and such things as cakes and fruits are uncountable. The laypeople seldom eat fish or meat. Most of the countries produce 210c
much nonglutinous rice but little millet and no glutinous millet at all. There are sweet melons and sugarcane, and taros are abundant. Okra is scarce, but rape turnips are grown in sufficient quantities. The latter has black and white seeds, which have recently been translated into Chinese as "mustard seeds." The oil extracted from these seeds is edible in all countries. When we eat its leaves as a vegetable, we find the taste is just the same as that of a Chinese turnip; the difference is that its root is hard and tough. The seed is so large that it is bigger than a [Chinese] mustard seed. The change may have been caused by the change of soil, just as the orange tree may bear citrons when transplanted from one place to another. At Nālandā I discussed this perplexing matter with the Dhyāna master Wuxing, but we could not clarify the matter in our debate. Again, the people of all five parts of India do not eat different minced condiments made of ginger, garlic, or leek, nor do they eat lettuce and the like. Therefore, they do not suffer from bellyaches. Their stomachs and intestines are soft and comfortable, and free from the trouble of becoming hard and inelastic.

In the ten islands of the South Seas, the offerings of food on festival days are still more substantially and liberally prepared. On the first day, a piece of betel nut, some fragrant oil extracted from aconite, and a small quantity of crushed rice are placed on a leaf as a vessel, which then is set on a big plate and covered with a piece of white kapok cloth. Water contained in a golden bottle is dripped on the ground before the plate as a signal to invite the monks, who are asked to anoint themselves and take a bath before noontime on the day after the following day. After noontime on the following day, amid the music of drum-beating and the offering of fragrant flowers, a holy image is carried either in a canopied carriage or in an imperial palanquin with streamers and banners fluttering in the sun. Monks and lay followers of the Dharma hurry like scudding clouds to the house of the donor, where a tent with curtains has been pitched for the occasion. The golden or bronze image is brilliantly decorated in a beautiful manner and anointed with aromatic paste. It is placed in a basin, and the people bathe it in scented water with devotion. After having been wiped clean with a piece of perfumed cotton cloth, it is taken to the main hall of the house. As incense is burned and lamps lit in profusion, the people begin to sing eulogistic hymns. Then the chief monk recites the *dānagāthā* for the sake of the donor to explain the merits of alms-giving. After that the monks are invited to come out of the hall to wash their hands and mouths, and then they are entertained with sugar water and sufficient betel nuts. After this, the assembly of monks breaks up and departs.

When noontime is approaching on the third day, the donor goes to the monastery and announces respectfully that the time [for the invitation] has come. The monks, after taking baths, are led to the donor's house. The holy image is set up again and bathed briefly, but there are twice the flowers, incense, and music of beating drums as the previous morning. All offerings are placed before the image, and five or ten maidens, or sometimes boys according to circumstances, stand solemnly on each side of the image, holding in their hands thuribles or golden bathing jugs or incense or lamps or fresh flowers or white chauris. The people come with toilet sets placed on dressing tables and mirrors contained in cases and the like to offer to the image of the Buddha. When I asked them the meaning of their action, they replied that it was in the cause of acquiring blessedness, and said that if they did not make offerings now, how could they expect to gain any rewards in the future? Logically speaking, theirs is a good action.

Next, a monk is invited to sing hymns while kneeling before the image of the Buddha. Then two more monks are separately invited, each taking a seat to one side of the image, to recite a brief scripture of one or half a page. Sometimes they sanctify an image of the Buddha by marking out the pupils of the image, so as to acquire superior happiness. Then they return to whichever side as they please, and fold up their *kāṣāya*s by fastening the two front corners together. After washing their hands, they are ready to take the meal. (Yijing's running note: *Kāṣāya* is a Sanskrit word, meaning the color of *gandha* [pounded sandalwood], and as it has no etymological connection with the Chinese language, why should one take the trouble to transliterate it with two Chinese characters to denote the monks' robes? According to the textual terms of the Vinaya, all three robes worn by a monk are known as *cīvara* [a monk's dress].) The manner of preparing for the meal, such as daubing the ground with cow's dung, examining water, washing the monks' feet, taking and serving the food, are generally the same as in India, except that they also eat the three kinds of pure meat. They generally sew leaves into plates as large as half a mat to keep one or two *dou* (one *dou* equals ten liters) of cooked nonglutinous rice on each plate, or else smaller receptacles are made to contain one or two *sheng* (one *sheng* equals one liter) of rice, which is brought to the monks and handed to them. Then various other kinds of food, twenty or thirty items, are served to the monks. This is in the case of a meal prepared by a poor and humble household. If it is done by a royal family or rich people, bronze plates and bowls and leaf vessels as large as a mat are used to contain more than a hundred varieties of food and drink. Even the kings give up their noble position of dignity and call themselves servants so as to serve food to the monks with perfect respect and veneration. 211a

The monks must accept without rejection whatever amount of food is offered to them. If they took just enough food to satisfy their hunger, the donor would feel displeased. He feels pleased only when he sees that too much food is being served. Four or five *sheng* of cooked rice and two or three plates of pancakes and fruits are offered to each monk, and the donor's relatives and neighbors may help prepare the meal by contributing rice or cakes. There is more than one dish of soup and vegetables for each partaker of the meal, and the leftover food for each monk is sufficient to feed three or four persons. In the case of a sumptuous meal, even ten persons cannot consume the remaining food left by one monk. All the remains of a meal are put at the disposal of the monks, who may order their servants to carry the food away with them.

But the ceremony of feasting the monks in the Divine Land of China is different from that of India in the west. In China, whatever food is left over is gathered by the donor, and the monks are not expected to take it away at will. Therefore, the monks should act according to the circumstances, be content with what they have, and not bring disgrace on themselves, so that they will not be unworthy of the good mind of the donor in alms-giving. But if the donor has made up his mind not to gather the remaining food and has invited the monks to take it away, they may then do what is suitable for the occasion.

After the monks have finished their meal and have washed their hands and mouths, the remaining food is cleared away and the ground swept clean. Flowers are scattered and lamps lit, while incense is burned to make the air aromatic, and what is to be presented to the monks is arranged before them. Then perfume paste, about the size of a seed of the Chinese parasol tree, is distributed to the monks, who rub their hands with it to make them fragrant and clean. Next, betel nuts and nutmegs mixed with cloves and camphor are offered to them. When chewed, this renders the mouth fragrant and also helps digestion and cures heart disease. These aromatic and medicinal things must be washed with pure water and wrapped in fresh leaves before they are handed to the monks.

The donor then goes to the chief monk, or approaches a competent teacher, and pours water from the spout of a bottle into a
211b basin, so that the water flows out incessantly like a slender copper stick. The teacher, with flowers in his hand, receives the trickling water while he recites the *dānagāthā*. He must first recite the verses spoken by the Buddha and then those composed by other

persons. He may recite as many or as few verses as he wishes, according to the time he has at his disposal. He must mention the name of the donor, praying for wealth and happiness for him and wishing to transfer the happy reward of good deeds done in the present to the deceased predecessors, to the emperors and princes, as well as to the *nāga*s (serpent demons) and spirits. He also wishes for rich harvests in the country, for the people and other creatures to live in peace, and for the noble teaching of Śākyamuni Buddha to be everlasting. The *gāthā,* which I have translated in some other place, is the blessing uttered by the World-honored One when he was living in the world. After the meal is over, the *Dakṣiṇāgāthā* (verse of alms-giving) must be recited. Such is the ceremony of giving alms. A *dakṣiṇīya* is one who is worthy to be honored with alms. Therefore, the Holy One laid down the rule that after each meal the monks should recite one or two *dānagāthā*s to recompense the donor for his bounteousness. (Yijing's running note: The word "donor" is a translation of the Sanskrit term *dānapati. Dāna* means alms and *pati,* a lord. The Chinese term *tan-yue,* indicating that by practicing alms-giving one may get across the stream of poverty, is not a correct translation of the Sanskrit word, in spite of the good interpretation. It is also incorrect to transliterate *dakṣiṇā* as *da-chen.*) If we do not do so, we are not only acting contrary to the holy teachings, but we shall also be unworthy of the food we have consumed. Begging for the remains of a meal is sometimes practiced.

Then gifts are distributed, or a "wishing tree" is made and presented to the monks, or a golden lotus flower is manufactured as an offering to the image of the Buddha. There are fresh flowers in knee-high heaps and enough white kapok cloth to fill a couch. After midday a sermon is occasionally delivered on a short scripture, and the monks sometimes disperse at nightfall. At the time of departure, they exclaim *"Sādhu!"* and also *"Anumoda." Sādhu* means "Well done!" and *anumoda* is translated as "I rejoice at what is being done!" When gifts are presented to others or to oneself, one should utter the same expressions. Both the one who presents the gifts and the one who praises the action with joy will gain bliss in the same way. Such is the general custom of the monks receiving offerings of food in the ten islands of the South Seas.

People of the middle class extend an invitation with the presentation of betel nuts to the monks on the first day. On the second day an image of the Buddha is bathed when it is nearly noontime, and the meal is finished at midday, while preaching is held in the evening. The poorer people either offer some tooth wood to invite the monks on the first day and simply prepare a meal on the following day, or they approach the monks and express their wish to invite them without further ceremony.

But the custom is different among the Hu tribes of the north, in countries such as Tukhāra and Suri. There the donor first presents a flower canopy as an offering to the *caitya* (temple), and then the monks go round the holy object while asking a precentor to say the prayers in their entirety before they take the meal. How the flower canopy looks has been described in the *Xi-fang-ji (A Record of the West).*

Although the ceremonies for offering food to the monks may be simple or elaborate in different countries, and the dishes served may be rich or scant, the monks' regulations, such as those on the preservation of purity or the way of eating food with one's fingers,
211c and the major monastic rules are much the same. Some of the monks practice the *dhūta* (ascetic) disciplines, living by begging for food and wearing only the three robes. If such a monk is invited and offered gold and valuables, he simply discards them like mucus or saliva and retires to live in a lonely forest. But in China in the east, the custom is that when a donor wishes to entertain some monks with a meal, he simply dispatches an invitation card to them. Even on the morning of the following day, he does not go in person to invite the monks. When compared with the teachings of the Buddha, this practice seems short of cordiality. The lay disciples should be taught proper manners. When going to attend a reception, a monk should bring his filter with him, and the water for the use of the monks must be examined. After the meal, a monk

should chew tooth wood to clean his mouth. If there is any remnant food left in the mouth, the meal is considered unfinished, and even should he pass the whole night hungry, he will not be spared the guilt of taking food at irregular times [as he has food particles in his mouth]. I hope that we will make a study of the manner of eating in India and reconsider the customs prevalent in China. Then we may naturally know what is appropriate and what is inappropriate. As I do not have the leisure to give a full account of the matter, I leave it to the wise to ponder.

Once I wrote an essay, which reads as follows:

> The Supreme World-honored One, the Father of Great Compassion, having pity on those who are plunged in the sea of transmigration, tried hard to gain enlightenment for three great kalpas (eons), and, with the hope to guide them, he lived for seven dozens of years to spread his teachings. Considering that the foremost requirements for upholding the Dharma were food and clothing, he feared that this might give rise to worldly troubles, and therefore laid down strict rules and prohibitions. These regulations, which reflect the will of the Buddha, should be observed and practiced. But on the contrary, there are some monks who indiscreetly think themselves guiltless and do not know what sorts of eating might cause defilement. They observe only the one rule against sexual conduct, and say, "Since we are guiltless, why should we take the trouble to study the Vinaya rules? Eating and drinking, dressing and undressing are irrelevant. The Buddha's will is pointing out the Way leading directly to the gate of voidness." But how do they know that the Vinaya rules were not laid down at the will of the Buddha? It is out of mere assumption that they value one rule and disregard another. Their disciples follow their examples and never read or have a look at the Vinaya rules. When they have copied just two fascicles of books on the gate of voidness, they say that this doctrine covers all the

theories of the Tripiṭaka. They do not consider that each mouthful of food swallowed illegally might cause the suffering of drinking molten copper in hell. Do they also not know that each step taken carelessly might incur the misery of being a traitor?

The original intention of the bodhisattva is to keep the skin raft tight [so that we may cross the sea of rebirth]. We must not overlook any minor offense; then we may render this life the last one without further rebirth. It is right for us to practice both the Mahayana and the Hinayana doctrines in keeping with the instructions of the Compassionate World-honored One. What fault is there if we take precautions against minor offenses and gain insight into the great voidness, to accept all living beings and clarify their minds? For fear that [my fellow monks at home] may perplex themselves and misguide others, I just submit this incomplete information according to the Buddha's teachings in the hope that they may draw inferences from it and gain complete knowledge. The Dharma of voidness is true and not false, but this is not a reason to disregard the Vinaya texts. It befits us to recite the Vinaya rules and make a confession to clear away our faults every fortnight. One should always advise and exhort the disciples to worship the Buddha three times a day. The Buddha-dharma is declining in the world day by day, and I have noticed that what I saw in my childhood was totally different from what I see now in my old age. Since we have witnessed the present situation, we must be more careful about our behavior. Eating and drinking are, however, a burden to us. They are our constant necessity, but I hope those who respect the Buddha will not disregard his holy teachings.

Let me repeat it:

212a Out of the eighty thousand holy teachings, only one or two are most important. Outwardly one should conform to the

> worldly way, while inwardly one should concentrate on true wisdom. But what is the worldly way? It is observing the prohibitive rules and being guiltless. And what is true wisdom? It is the abandonment of both the faculty of sight and the object seen. One should follow the superior truth without any attachment, and do away with the entanglements of life arising from the chain of causality. One must diligently accumulate merit by practicing more good deeds, so as to realize the wonderful meaning of perfect truth. How can a monk falsely declare that he has attained the state of *bodhi* (enlightenment), while he has never studied the Tripiṭaka, knows neither the teachings nor the principles of the Dharma, and has committed sinful deeds as numerous as the grains of sand in the Ganges River? *Bodhi* means enlightenment, in which all illusions and entanglements are destroyed. There is neither birth nor death in the state known as eternal reality. How can we carelessly say that we are living in the Western Paradise, while we are actually staying in the sea of suffering? One who desires to realize the truth of eternity should observe the disciplinary rules with purity as a basis. One should guard against a tiny hole that might be punctured in the air bag, and take precautions against the major offenses, even though they might assume such a small shape as a needle's eye. Of all the great grievances, the foremost are mainly caused by food and clothing. If one follows the Buddha's teachings, one will not be far from gaining spiritual liberation, and if one disregards the noble words, one will surely be submerged in the sea of rebirth for a long time.

I have so far related the rightful practices and briefly described some examples of our predecessors. All this is based on the holy regulations; none comes out of my own views and intentions. I hope my readers will not feel displeased at my straightforward statement, and that it may be useful for those who are far away from me. If I do not make an exact statement and submit it to my readers, who will discern what is refined and what is vulgar?

End of Fascicle One

Fascicle Two

10. The Requirements for Raiment and Food

It may be observed that the corporeal body depends upon food and clothing for its maintenance, while the perfect wisdom of no rebirth is manifested through the truth of voidness. If one makes use of food and clothing in a way contrary to proper manners, one will incur blame on oneself step by step; and if the concentrated mind loses its proper course, one will get into perplexity thought after thought. Therefore, those who wish to realize spiritual liberation in the course of using food and clothing should use them in accordance with the holy words of the Buddha, and those who try to practice the truth with a concentrated mind should conform with the teachings of former sages in order to concentrate their 212b
minds. Looking down upon the life below, one sees that it is but a dungeon for those who have gone astray. Gazing up to the shore of nirvana, one beholds the open gate of enlightenment and tranquility. Only by doing so may one pull the boat of Dharma to the shore in the sea of suffering and hold up the torch of wisdom during the long period of darkness. As regards the regulations about wearing robes and how to eat and drink, observance and violation are expressly prescribed in the Vinaya texts; even a beginner in the Dharma knows what is a grave offense and what is a light one. This is, however, a matter, whether meritorious or demeritorious, that concerns only individual persons, and we need not take the trouble to argue about it here. There are some who behave against the Vinaya rules and yet guide others in their conduct. There are some others who hold that usage gives rise to practices, that, whether they are right or wrong, are considered regular and

faultless. Some others argue that the Buddha was born in the west, where the monks follow the custom and manners of the west, while as we are monks living in the east, we should follow the rules and regulations of the east. "How can we," they would say, "change the elegant dress of the Divine Land of China and accept the peculiar customs of India?" It is for people holding such views that I have made this rough statement, so that they can weigh the matter by themselves.

As the regulations concerning clothing are the guiding principles of homeless monks, it befits me to give a full description of the style of their clothing. This should never be neglected or overlooked. The laps of the three robes worn by monks in all five parts of India are sewn together; only in China are they open without being stitched up. I myself have made inquiries in the northern countries of India where the Vinaya of the Dharmagupta School is prevalent and found that the openings of the robes are sewn together; nowhere are they left open. If a monk of India has obtained a Chinese religious robe, he would probably sew up the openings before he would wear it. The Vinaya texts of all the schools mention that the laps of the robes should be sewn and fastened together. There are strict rules about the six requisites of the monks, and the thirteen necessities are fully explained in the Vinaya texts. The following are the six requisites:

1. The *saṃghāṭī,* which is translated as "double robe."
2. The *uttarāsaṅga,* which is translated as "upper robe."
3. The *antarvāsa,* which is translated as "inner garment."

(These three garments are known as the *cīvara*. In the northern countries they are generally called the *kāṣāya* from their reddish color. However, this is not a technical term used in the Vinaya texts.)

4. The *pātra,* a begging bowl.
5. The *niṣīdana,* a cloth or mat for sitting or lying on.
6. The *parisrāvaṇa,* a filter.

A candidate for ordination must possess these six requisites.

The following are the thirteen necessities:

1. The *saṃghāṭī*.
2. The *uttarāsaṅga*.
3. The *antarvāsa*.
4. The *niṣīdana*.
5. An undergarment.
6. A substitute undergarment.
7. The *saṃkakṣikā* (a side-covering vest).
8. A substitute *saṃkakṣikā*.
9. A towel for wiping the body.
10. A towel for wiping the face.
11. A pinafore used when shaving one's hair.
12. A piece of cloth for covering itchy places.
13. A garment worn when decocting medicine.

A verse says:

Three robes and a sitting cloth, 212c
A couple of skirts and two side-covers,
Towels for wiping body and face, a pinafore for shaving,
A cloth to cover itches and a garb for decocting medicine.

These are the thirteen kinds of clothes which a monk is permitted to possess. Since there are established rules concerning clothing, one must use them in compliance with the Buddha's teaching. These thirteen articles should not be classed with other surplus belongings of a monk, but should be separately listed, clearly counted, and well preserved. When one receives any of these things, one may keep them, but one should not take the trouble to possess all that is given to one. As regards the surplus robes, a monk may dispose of them in different ways according to circumstances, but as for such things as woolen mattresses, blankets, mats, and the like, he may accept and use them only with the understanding that they are purposely committed to him by the givers.

Sometimes people speak of three robes and ten necessities, but it was the idea of some translators to divide the thirteen necessities into two groups; it is not in accordance with the Sanskrit texts. They speak separately of the three robes and list the ten articles apart from the robes. But they cannot give a full list of the ten articles, and thus cause groundless conjecture and guessing. If they interpret the word *shi* (meaning ten) as "miscellaneous," this is not the original meaning.

The garment for decocting medicine which the Buddha permitted the monks to keep should be made of a piece of silk about twenty feet long, or a whole roll of it. As one may fall ill at any time, it would be difficult to obtain such a garment in a hurry, and so a monk is permitted to make one beforehand and keep it. As this garment is needed in time of illness, it must not be used at random times.

The purpose of the gate of spiritual cultivation and benefiting living beings is universal salvation. Since men are of three grades of intelligence, they cannot be limited to only one way. The four dependences, the four actions, and the twelve ascetic practices are ordained for men of superior intelligence. Keeping a room for one's own use and accepting gifts of the thirteen necessities are good for monks of both medium and inferior intelligence, so that those who have fewer desires will be spared the embarrassment of having surplus daily requisites, and those who wish to have more will not fret at deficiency. Great is the compassionate father who skillfully answers the needs of men of all grades of intelligence and is a good teacher for human and heavenly beings, with the title of Guide of Men.

The assertion that one hundred and one things may be offered to meet a monk's physical needs is not found in the Vinaya texts of the four schools. Although allusions to it are made in some scriptures, it was mentioned only on special occasions. Even a wealthy layman does not possess more than fifty household articles. How can a monk, who is detached from worldly entanglements, be allowed, on the contrary, to own more than a hundred things? One may judge by reason to know whether it is permissible or not.

As regards the use of fine and tough silk, it is permitted by the holy Buddha. Why should one forcibly prohibit the use of it to make things knottier? I judge that the intention to simplify things rendered matters more complicated. In all five parts of India, monks of the four schools wear [silk robes]. Why should we reject silk, which is easy to procure, and try to obtain fine cotton, which is difficult to seek? Isn't it a hindrance that obstructs the Way to the utmost? Such a rule belongs to the class of prohibitions that were not laid down by the Buddha but were enforced by others. This caused some meddlesome observers of the Vinaya rules to swell their self-conceit and look down upon others.

Those venerable ones who seek nothing and have few desires, being humble-minded inwardly and modest outwardly, would say that theirs is the best way to cover oneself; what else would it be? They mean that silk is produced by injuring life, which hurts the mind of compassion extremely. Out of pity for living beings, it is 213a
logical to not use silk. If that is so, then the clothes we wear and the food we eat are in most cases produced by injury to life. If we did not pay attention to mole crickets and earthworms, why should we be specially mindful of chrysalises and silkworms? If one wishes to protect all animate beings, then there will be no means of sustaining oneself, and why should one forsake life without a good reason? From logical inference, we may conclude that such an idea is impractical. Those monks who refrain from eating ghee and curds, and from wearing leather shoes and silk or floss robes, are people of the class mentioned above.

Regarding the question of killing, if a life is destroyed intentionally, it is then considered a karmic deed [that will produce its due effect], but if it is done unintentionally, the Buddha said, it is not considered an evil deed. The three kinds of pure meat are designated as to be eaten without incurring blame. If one does not act in conformity with the spirit of this rule, one commits but a slight offense. [To argue it by means of a syllogism, we may raise the proposition that] eating pure meat is guiltless, for the reason, which is accepted by both parties to the argument, that the act is done without the intention of killing. If we add an example to the syllogism, the statement will be clear and manifest. Since the reason and example indicate that the act is guiltless, the proposition becomes self-apparent. The syllogism has made the statement perspicuous, and moreover, it is the golden saying of the Buddha. Why should we then take the trouble to give it more strained interpretations? They simply made people as confused as the miswriting of "five hundred" for "five days" through a slip of the author's pen and the erroneous reading of "three pigs" for "earth-pig," which was transmitted by those who believed the words to be true.

Such an action as begging for live cocoons and witnessing the destruction of the silkworms is something that even a lay scholar would not do, let alone a monk, who aspires to gain liberation from the world. To quote this as a proof, I consider it utterly inadmissible. If a donor comes with a pure mind to present a silk robe to a monk, the monk should utter the word *"Anumoda"* and accept it to clothe his body so that he may cultivate virtue, without incurring any blame.

In the five parts of India, the religious garment may be stitched or sewn at one's discretion, disregarding whether the threads of the cloth are lengthwise or crosswise. The time for making it does not exceed three or five days. One bolt of silk can be cut into one garment of seven stripes and another of five stripes. The inside patches are three fingers wide, while the peripheral edges are one inch broad. These edges have three rows of stitching, and the inside patches are all sewn together. As these garments are used for performing daily duties or holding ceremonies, why should we make them look fine and exquisite?

The intention of those who wear rag robes is to simplify things. They may either gather cast-off rags from rubbish heaps or pick up abandoned clothes at a cemetery. Whenever they have obtained such rags, they sew them up into robes to protect themselves against cold and hot weather.

Some people say that what is mentioned as sleeping articles in the Vinaya texts is included in the category of the three robes.

When they see that the use of silk from wild cocoons is prohibited [for making sleeping articles], they hold the view that the robes also should not be made of silk. Thus they try hard to seek cotton cloth, not knowing that in the original texts "sleeping article" actually means a mattress and that the word *kauśeya* is the name for silkworm. When the silk fiber is woven into silk cloth, it is also known by the same name. As it is costly material, making it into a mattress is not allowed.

There are two ways of making a mattress. One way is to sew a piece of cloth to make a bag and fill it with wool. Another is to weave silk thread into a mattress which is something like a carpet. It is two cubits wide, four cubits long, and may be thick or thin according to the season. Begging for a mattress is forbidden, but if it is given as alms, it may be accepted without incurring blame. If it were completely banned, it would be a grave matter, and a strict rule should have been laid down against its use. Such mattresses are not the same as the three robes.

Again, what is mentioned in the Vinaya as "right livelihood"
mainly concerns the procurement of subsistence. The plowing and 213b
weeding of fields should be done in the proper way, while sowing and planting must not be done in a manner which violates the guiding principles of the religion. If food is taken according to the regulations, it will not give rise to any blame. Only then may one say that by building up the body one can increase happiness.

According to the teaching of the Vinaya, in the cultivation of paddy fields, the Sangha (community of monks) must share the crops with the monastic servants and may also share them with other families, all of whom may get one-sixth of the produce. The Sangha provides farm cattle and land only, and is responsible for nothing else. The division of crops may be appropriately adjusted according to circumstances.

Most of the monasteries in the west follow the system mentioned above. There are some avaricious monks who do not share the produce in proportion with others, but employ male and female slaves and personally manage the farming business. *Bhikṣu*s who abide by the disciplinary rules refuse to eat the food produced by such monks because they think that such monks, by personally running a farm, support themselves by improper livelihood. By ordering about the hired men who work in the fields, they inevitably arouse their resentment, and digging the earth to plant seeds as well as plowing land are liable to injure ants and other insects. One's daily ration is no more than one *sheng* of grain; who can make it stand for a hundred evil deeds? Hence an honest and upright monk is disgusted with the cumbersome task of farming. He abandons it and goes far away with his pot and bowl to sit alone in a quiet forest and takes pleasure in the company of birds and deer. Being away from the hubbub of pursuing fame and gain, he cultivates the calm of nirvana.

If a monk manages a business to gain profit for the Sangha, it is permitted by the Vinaya, but he is not allowed to cultivate land and injure living things. Nothing is more harmful to insects and more obstructive to good deeds than the cultivation of land. The guilt and wrong livelihood related to the cultivation of ten *qing* (one *qing* equals 6.6666 hectares) of land have not been enumerated in any books, but people have repeatedly taken the trouble to waste pen and ink in writing about the rules concerning the three faultless and rightful robes. Alas! I can tell this matter only to those who have faith; it is difficult for me to discuss it with those who are skeptical because I fear those who transmit the Dharma may still persistently adhere to their own views.

When I arrived at Tāmralipti for the first time, I saw a square field outside the monastery. Some laymen suddenly came there to fetch vegetables, which they divided into three portions, giving one portion to the Sangha and taking two away for themselves. I did not understand what was going on, and inquired of the Venerable Mahāyānadīpa about their intention. He said in reply, "The monks of this monastery are mostly observers of the disciplinary rules. As they are not allowed by the Great Sage to cultivate land themselves, they rent the land to others and take a share of the crops for food." In this manner they could sustain their lives by right livelihood without involving themselves with worldly connections, as they were free from the fault of destroying living things through plowing and irrigating the fields. I also saw a *bhikṣu* (mendicant), who was the director of monastic affairs, inspect the water from a well every morning. If there was no insect in the water, it was used. Once life was found in it, it had to be filtered before being used. I also saw that whenever anything, even as small as a piece of a vegetable, was given by outsiders, the monks had to ask the permission of the Sangha before they might use it. I also saw that no controller was appointed in the monastery; when anything happened, a meeting was convened to make a decision. If a monk acted according to his own will and made decisions as he pleased, or treated others favorably or unfavorably regardless of the opinion of the Sangha, he was called a *kulapati* (layman) and expelled by the Sangha.

I also saw that when the nuns had to go to a monastery, they 213c
had to make an announcement before they started to proceed there. When the monks had to go to a nunnery, they had to make an inquiry before going there. When monks wished to go out of the monastery, they had to go out in twos, and when they had to go to a layman's house on business, they might, with the permission of the Sangha, go in a company of four. I also saw that on the four fast days of each month, the monks of the whole monastery assembled in the evening to listen to a recitation of the disciplinary rules, which they observed with deep deference.

I also witnessed the following incident: Once a junior monk ordered his boy attendant to send two *sheng* of rice to the wife of a servant because of the junior monk's illicit relations with the woman. This matter was reported to the Sangha, and the monk was summoned to answer questions. In the course of interrogation, the three admitted their misbehavior. Although the junior monk did not commit the evil act, he was ashamed of himself, withdrew his name from the list of monks, and went away from the monastery forever. His teacher asked somebody to send his clothing and other things to him. Such is the clerical law which all the monks observed. They need not take the trouble to go to a secular court of justice for a settlement.

I also saw that once a woman came to the monastery, but she did not enter the chambers. She just spoke with the monks in the corridor for a short moment and went away. I also saw that in the monastery there was a *bhikṣu* by the name of Rāhulamitra, who was then about thirty years old. His conduct was unusually perfect and his fame was high and far reaching. Every day he read the *Ratnakūṭa-sūtra,* which consisted of seven hundred stanzas. He was well versed in the Buddhist texts of the Tripiṭaka, and was thoroughly conversant with those secular books, the four Vedas. He was honored as an elder in the eastern part of the Land of Saints. Since he was fully ordained, he had never spoken face to face with a woman; even when his mother or elder sister came, he would come out just to have a look at them. When I asked him why he behaved like that, since it was not the holy teaching, he said in reply, "I am a man of much carnal passion by nature, and if I did otherwise, I could not stop its source. Although [to speak with women] is not prohibited by the Holy One, what is wrong if my behavior is meant to prevent evil desires?"

I also saw that learned monks who were well versed in the holy texts of any one of the three collections were lodged in the best chambers and provided with servants to wait upon them. They gave lectures regularly and were exempted from routine monastic duties. When they went out, they mostly rode in palanquins, but never on horseback. I also saw that when a guest monk came to the monastery for the first time, the Sangha would provide him with good food for five days, so that he could rest and recover from fatigue. After that he lived like other ordinary monks. If he was a good person, the Sangha might invite him to stay and allow him to spend the summer retreat that year with a supply of bedding. If he was not a learned man, he would be treated like the other regular monks. Only those who were well learned were treated with the arrangements mentioned above, with their names written in the monastic register just like the original resident monks.

I also saw that when a man came with a good mind, he would be asked his purpose, and if he came to become a monk, the Sangha would shave his hair. His name would have nothing more to do with the king's census register, as the monks kept their own registration books. Afterwards, if he violated the Vinaya rules and committed misdeeds, he would be expelled with the sound of a *ghaṇṭā* (bell). Thus the monks would examine each other and see to it that faults were nipped in the bud and not allowed to grow up gradually in the course of time.

I should say with a sigh that when I was in the Divine Land of China, I thought of myself as knowing the Vinaya well, and little imagined that after coming here to India, I should have found myself ignorant of the subject. Had I not come to the west, how could 214a
I have seen such correct rules and regulations? Some of these rules are laid down by the monks of the monastery and some are specially made for the rectification of the mind, while the rest are found in the Vinaya texts, which are important for the maintenance of the Buddha's teachings in this period of the decay of the Dharma.

All these are the rules of the Bālāha Monastery at Tāmralipti, but at Nālandā Monastery the regulations are still stricter. Thus over three thousand monks lived there, with a fief of more than two hundred villages, which were offered to them as alms by the kings and monarchs of successive dynasties. The uninterrupted prosperity of the monastery is due to nothing else but the observance of the Vinaya rules by the monks.

I have never seen [in India] that a secular official would sit in the middle of the audience hall of his yamen, while the monks stand aside in a row, bullied, slighted, called and shouted to just like ordinary laymen. The monks [in China] run about, seldom feeling tired on the way, to see off a leaving official and welcome the new one. If the imperial inspector does not visit the monastery, they go to the government house to seek a livelihood, without regarding whether it is in the cold or the hot season.

A man becomes a homeless monk because he wishes to free himself from worldly entanglements, so as to give up the hazardous way of the five fears and follow the safe thoroughfare of the eightfold right path. Why should one be again involved in mundane affairs and be caught once more in the net of immorality? If so, how can we fulfill our wish of achieving perfect calm? It may be said that in that way we are acting entirely in contradiction to spiritual emancipation and not in concordance with quietude. It is only reasonable that we should practice the twelve *dhūta* (ascetic ways of living) and own only the thirteen articles of necessity to sustain our lives according to circumstances. We should wash away old habits, repay the great bounty of our teachers and of the Sangha and our parents, and requite the heavenly beings and *nāga*s, as well as the lords and emperors, for their deep compassion. In this way we may well follow the laws of the Guide of Men and become rightly fit for the path of spiritual cultivation and exhortation. In the course of discussing the preservation of life, I have mentioned actual practices. I hope my virtuous readers will not feel that my discussion is dull and tedious.

The distinctions between the four schools are marked by the way the monks wear their undergarments. The monks of the Sarvāstivāda School double-fold their undergarments outwards on both sides, while the monks of the Mahāsāṃghika School stuff the right piece of the undergarment into the left side and press it in tightly, so that it will not get loose. The women of India in the west wear their skirts in just the same way as the monks of the Mahāsāṃghika School. The way that the monks of the Sthavira and Sāṃmitīya Schools wear their undergarments is similar to that of the Mahāsāṃghika School, except that they turn the edge outwards and press it to one side. The make of girdle is also different. The nuns wear their robes in the same manner as the monks of their respective schools, with no difference at all.

But the Chinese monks' *saṃkakṣikā*s (outer garments), which are worn over only one shoulder, and their square skirts, trousers, leg sheaths, loose gowns with huge sleeves, and short jackets are all contrary to the original rules. Not only do their robes have

sleeves similar to those on laymen's clothes and cover the whole back closely, even their manner of wearing them is not in concordance with the Vinaya rules. Both wearing and using such garments are blameworthy. Some Chinese monks attired in such dress came to India in the west, and the local people laughed at them. As they were ashamed of themselves, they tore their clothes to pieces for miscellaneous use, because it is unwarranted for a monk to wear any such garments. If I kept silence without saying anything, people would not be able to know about it. Although I wished to speak outright, I feared that my hearers would bear resentment towards me. Hence, I tried to express my superficial views in this composition of mine, but I hesitated to proceed or hold back. I wish that the wise ones will make a careful study so as to know 214b
about the original rules concerning clothing.

In India the garments worn by the laypeople, officials, and noblemen of higher castes consist of only two pieces of fine white cotton cloth, while the poor and low-caste people merely have one piece of cotton cloth. The homeless monks possess only the three robes and the six requisites, and only those who take delight in owning more things use the thirteen necessities. In China the monks are not allowed to wear garments with two sleeves and a whole back, but the fact is that they follow Chinese customs and talk falsely about things Indian.

Now I will give a brief description of the people and their costume in Jambudvīpa and the various islands on the border of the sea. From Mahābodhi eastward to Lin-yi, there are more than twenty countries extending up to the southern boundary of Huanzhou. If we proceed to the southwest, we reach the sea. In the north, Kaśmīra is the limit, while in the South Seas there are more than ten countries, including the island of Siṃhala. In all these countries the people wear two pieces of *kambala* (a woolen loincloth), which is neither cut nor sewn up, without a girdle. It is simply a wide piece of cloth about two fathoms long, put around the waist to cover the lower parts. Beyond India at the edge of the great sea are the countries of the Persians and the Tajiks, where the people wear shirts and trousers, while in the country of the naked, the people wear no dress at all, both men and women being stark naked. Further away from Kaśmīra, the various Hu peoples, such as the Tibetans and the Turks of Suli, dress in roughly the same way. They do not wear *kambalas*, but use felt and fur, and have little *karoāsa* (cotton), which is used only occasionally. As it is a cold region, shirts and trousers are regularly used.

Among these countries, except those of the Persians, the naked people, the Tibetans, and the Turks, where no Buddhism was known originally, all follow the Buddha's teachings. Even in the lands where shirts and trousers are used, the people do not bathe themselves clean; hence the people of the five parts of India are proud of their own cleanliness and sublimity. But so far as cultural personality and refinement, etiquette in meeting friends, the culinary art, magnanimity of kindness, and righteousness are concerned, no country excels China in the east. The monks in China, however, do not preserve the purity of food, and neither do they wash after going to the latrine, nor chew willow twigs to cleanse their teeth. In these matters they are different from the western regions. Some monks hold that it is faultless to wear improper garments and quote a passage from the *Saṃkṣipta-śāsana-vinaya-sūtra* which says, "What is considered impure in this place, may be regarded as pure in other places, where it may be practiced without fault." This passage is mistranslated and the correct meaning is not so, as I have pointed out elsewhere.

For a *bhikṣu* in China, garments other than the three robes are not allowable by the sacred rules. Since it is faulty to put on extra garments, it is reasonable not to use them. In a warm country like India one may use only one unlined garment through all the seasons of the year, but in a cold country with snowy hills, how could one live in health if one wished to discard [warm clothes]? It is the sincere word of the Buddha that we should keep our body in ease and our work in progress, while the practice of self-torture and immoderate exertion is the teaching of heretics. Now what should we take or reject?

The Buddha permitted the use of the *repa* garment, which is commonly worn in cold countries and is sufficient to keep the body warm. How can it be said to be a hindrance to the practice of the 214c Way? The Sanskrit word *repa* may be interpreted as "abdomen covering cloth." I will give a brief description of how it is made. Cut a piece of cloth so as to make it without a back, leaving one shoulder bare. No sleeve is attached to one side. It is only one piece of cloth, just big enough to put on. The shoulder sleeve, which is not wide, is on the left side, and it is not fitting to make it wide and large. It is tied up on the right side with strings so that no wind will waft into the garment. It may be stuffed with a large quantity of cotton wool to make it thick and warm. Sometimes the right side of this sort of underwear is sewn right up to the armpit, so that it has to be slipped on over the head. Such is the proper way of making this garment which I have seen in the west. Most of the monks coming from the Hu regions brought along and wore this kind of garment, but I never saw such clothes at Nālandā, because it is in a hot country where the people do not use them. From this we may know that monks are allowed to wear this kind of garment in cold countries. The old clothes, which are bare at the back, originally followed the example of this garment. But an extra piece of cloth added to the right side makes the garment lose its former style. If one does not make a garment according to the established rules, one is sure to commit an offense against the Dharma.

As regards the *repa* garment, it is for wrapping the abdomen to protect it in the severe cold season, while the thick mantle which is worn over the whole body is warm enough to prevent frostbite. When worshiping the Buddha's image in a shrine hall, or in the presence of a senior monk, one should always keep one shoulder bare; to cover it incurs guilt. As it is for the sake of getting rid of encumbrances that one becomes a homeless monk, and moreover, as a charcoal fire is always kept burning in the living quarters during the winter season, there is no need for a monk to put on superfluous clothes. In case of illness, when it is necessary to wear more clothes, one may do so at one's own discretion, but one should not act against the rules.

In China, however, the severe cold may pierce the body, and if one did not put on warm clothes, one would certainly die of enervation. Since we are all alike involved in suffering, it is reasonable to extend salvation to all people. The square skirt and the robe that leaves one shoulder bare distinguish a monk from a layman, but the *repa* garment is to be worn only temporarily during the cold season of winter. From this we may know that it was not originally designed for monks to wear, but that for the sake of protecting our lives we are permitted to use it, as the wheels of a cart need oiling. We should feel deep shame at being obliged to do so, and the best thing is not to wear it. Other clothes, such as loose gowns, leg sheaths, trousers, and shirts should by no means be allowed for regular use. As soon as the severe cold season is over, it is not fitting to wrap the whole body in such clothes. One should change them for a robe that leaves one shoulder uncovered, as it is actually not permissible for a monk to wear them. In this way we may get the gist and be rid of the superfluities of the matter, acting according to the true teachings of the Buddha. One may act freely only for oneself; if one teaches in that way, I fear one will mislead others.

If we could change the old course and strike out on a new path, we might then continue the line [left by Bodhidharma] at Shaoshi Mountain and be as lofty as Vulture Peak. We might sit side by side [with the sages] in the city of Rājagṛha and transmit the Dharma to the country of the Emperor so that we might protect it together. Thus the Yellow River might mingle its pure water with the Lake of Mucilinda. The slender-leaved willow would shine simultaneously with the bodhi tree, which would thrive until the field of mulberry trees changes [into the sea]. The glory would last until the kalpa-stone is completely wiped away. How marvelous it would be! Let us strive to attain this goal!

But now the Sun of the Buddha has sunk and only his teaching is left behind in this period of termination. If we practice his teaching, it is just as if we are living in the presence of the Great Teacher, but if we act against his teaching, various faults will be perpetrated. The Buddha, therefore, said in a sutra, "If my precepts are followed, it shall be just as if I am living in this world."

Someone may say that since the virtuous people of old did not say anything about such things, why should we, men of a later time, change the convention? It is not correct to say so. For it is 215a
the Dharma, and not any man, upon which we depend; this point has been extensively expounded in the Buddha's doctrine. Research into the Vinaya texts will show that monks may take only such clothing and food as are not tainted by violations of the precepts. It is not hard to know a thing, but to practice it is difficult. If a man fails to practice what he has learned, why should the teacher be blamed?

Let me repeat it:

For all living beings,
Food and clothing are most important.
They are the cangue and shackles
Keeping us in the field of rebirth.
By following the holy word and rules,
One may get freedom from the world.
To act in one's own way
Involves trouble and faults.
Let the wise men know
Retribution is instant.
One should be unstained like jade in mire
Or a lotus growing out of muddy water.
When the eight airs have left the body,
The five fears give no more trouble.
Clothing is only for covering the body;
Food is merely for sustaining life.
Fix your mind on attaining emancipation;
Never wish to be reborn as a man or a god.
Practice austerities to the end of life;

Spend your years saving all living beings.
Give up the unreality of the nine happy abodes;
Aspire to the perfection and firmness of the ten stages.
Try to be qualified to receive alms fit for the five hundred
arhats
And competent to give benefit and welfare to the three
thousand worlds.

11. How to Wear the Robes

Now I will give a description, according to the Vinaya, about how to wear the three robes and make loops and fasteners. Take a religious robe that is five cubits long, and fold it into three layers. A patch of cloth about five finger-widths square is fixed at the pleat on the shoulder about four or five finger-widths within the border of the robe. The four sides of the patch are stitched on the robe. A small hole is made with an awl in the center to fix the loop, which is made of silk braid or a piece of silk cloth and is about the size of the loops of an ordinary shirt. It is two fingers long, tied into a love knot. The remainder should be cut off. One end of the loop is then put into the hole and drawn out to the other side of the robe. It is pulled back crosswise to form two loops. The inner part of the fastener is at the pleated part of the robe in front of the chest. The fasteners at the border of the robe are fixed in the same way as those fixed on a shirt. Such is the method of fixing fasteners on a robe. This is only a rough description which I am submitting to my readers for the time being. If one wishes to know the actual method in detail, one has to learn about it face to face from a teacher. Loops and fasteners are also fixed at the lower part of the robe. As the monks are permitted by the Buddha to wear their robes upside down at will, a loop and a fastener are fixed separately at the two lower corners, about eight finger-widths from the border of the robe. Monks are required, at mealtime, to fasten the reversely folded corners together before the chest. This is an essential point.

When one is in a monastery or in the presence of an assembly of monks, one must not use the strings and fasteners, or cover both shoulders with the robe. But when one is going out of the monastery or entering a layman's house, one must tie up the fasteners. At other times one may just cover the shoulders. When one is in seclusion or performing monastic duties, one may put on the robe inside out at will. But in the honored presence of an image of the Buddha, one must dress properly and tidily, putting the right corner of the robe loosely over the left shoulder so that it hangs behind the back without falling on the arm. If one wishes to use the fastenings, one should cover both shoulders with the robe and then turn the fastenings inside to fall in back of the shoulder; one must not let them get loose. When the corner is put over the shoulder, the robe 215b
may go round the neck, and both one's hands may come out beneath the robe with the corner hanging in front. A lovely statue of King Aśoka, depicting him in a procession with an umbrella over him, is dressed in this manner. This is the way to wear the upper robe in an orderly manner according to the teaching of the Buddha.

The umbrella may be woven out of slender bamboo sticks, as thin as a bamboo vessel of only one layer. The size may be two or three feet in diameter at one's option. The center is made doubly thick to hold the handle, the length of which is in proportion to the circumference of the cover. The cover of the umbrella may be painted with a thin layer of lacquer. It may also be woven of reed. If paper is pasted inside the cover, in the way that rattan hats and the like are manufactured, it is made strong.

Although umbrellas have not been used in China before, it is desirable to make them. In a sudden shower, it protects our robes from getting wet, and in the heat of the blazing sun, it keeps us cool under its shade. To use an umbrella is in concordance with the Vinaya as well as beneficial to our bodies, and there is no harm in holding one. Many of the necessary things we have discussed here have not been used in China before.

One corner of the *kāṣāya* hangs in front like the trunk of an elephant. All Indian monks who came to China wore the robe in this fashion, because fine silk is so smooth that a robe made of it is liable to slip down the shoulder. Thus the correct way of dressing was replaced by a wrong manner. Afterwards, when the Tripiṭaka master of the Tang dynasty (Venerable Xuanzang) came back from India, he introduced wearing the robe with one corner hanging over the shoulder, but many of the elderly monks still disliked it. A bias towards persistence in old practices exists everywhere.

With regard to the three robes, if short fastenings are fixed on them instead of long ribbons, it is not considered a fault. Wearing a whole piece of cloth sideways as a skirt without a waist piece will save one the trouble of sewing and stitching. The water pot, the alms bowl, and all other belongings should be hung on the shoulders just below the armpits so that the strings will not intertwine. The strings should not be too long, just long enough to hang the objects over the shoulders. If the strings crossed before the chest, they would cause one to pant for breath. One must not do so, as it is not the original way of carrying things. I shall talk about the bag for carrying the alms bowl later.

The people of Suli and other places in the north often carry things crossing one another. This is a regional modification and was not a rule laid down by the Buddha. If one has an extra robe, one may first put it lengthwise over one shoulder and then cover both shoulders over the robe one is wearing and the alms bowl one is carrying.

When going to a monastery or repairing to a layman's house, one must go into the premises to put down the umbrella, and then untie the strings to hang up one's [extra] robe and alms bowl. The wall before a house is usually fixed with ivory hangers, so that visitors will not be in want of a place to hang their things. Other relevant matters will be related in Chapter Twenty-six on how to meet an old acquaintance.

As a *kāṣāya* made of thin silk is very slippery, it cannot easily stay on the shoulder, and when one is worshiping an image of the Buddha, it often falls to the ground. So it is better to use some less smooth stuff, such as rough silk or fine cotton cloth. As regards the *saṃkakṣikā,* i.e., the side-covering garment, it should be more than one cubit long in order to comply with the original rules. Then wearing this kind of garment, the right shoulder is bare and only the left one is covered. In the chamber one always wears this garment and a skirt, but when going out to salute honored ones, one has to put on other robes in addition.

As for how to wear the skirt, I will just give a brief account. According to the rules for making a skirt adopted by the 215c Sarvāstivāda School, the skirt is a piece of fine silk or cotton cloth, as the case may be, five cubits across by two cubits long. In India it is made unlined, while in China it may be lined as one pleases, and the length and width are as desired. After having put it around [the lower part of] the body, you pull it up to cover the navel. Hold the upper corner of the left flap of the skirt with your right hand, and pull it from the inside to reach the right side of the waist. The left flap of the upper robe is taken to cover the left side. (Yijing's running note: The right flap is the one near the right hand; the left flap, the one near the left hand.) Raise both ends of the skirt to make them even and twist them right in the middle into three folds. Then press them with both hands into the waist with all three folds turned back and twisted beneath. The two corners are raised three fingers higher and inserted inwards about three fingers down to the skirt itself. When the skirt is worn in this manner, it will stick to the body and will not fall off even if it is not tied with a belt. Then hook up the middle of the skirt with a waistband about five cubits long, and raise it up below the navel. Bind the skirt at the upper edge and stretch it to the back in double layers which are folded one upon the other and drawn to the front at the left and right sides. Hold both ends of the band, one in each hand, and press them fast on both sides. Then bind the waist three times with the two ends of the band. If it is too long, cut it short, and if it is not long enough, add some more to it. The ends of the band should not be stitched or adorned. This is the all-round way of wearing the skirt [known in Sanskrit as *parimaṇḍala-nivāsa,* translated into Chinese as the all-round way of wearing the skirt] which is the distinctive mark of the Sarvāstivāda School. The width of the waistband is about that of a finger. As regards the bootlace, the garter, and the like, they may be square or round. It is harmless to use them doubled up, but to use such a thing as hempen string is not allowed by the Vinaya texts.

When one sits in a small chair, or on a block of wood, one should hold up the lower corners of the skirt and press the edge of the skirt under the thighs with a quick movement just to cover the knees. It is harmless to leave the shins uncovered. The upper part of the skirt should cover the navel, and the lower part should reach the point four fingers above the ankles. Such is the manner of wearing the skirt in a layman's house, but in a monastery it is allowable to cover just the upper part of the shins. These limits were fixed by the Buddha, and no one should alter them at will. Should one purposely act against the Buddha's teachings to satisfy one's human fancies? If the skirt one wears is so long as to trail on the ground, one would spoil the pure gift presented by a devotee on the one hand, and on the other hand, would disregard the maxims of the Great Teacher. My remonstrance is sincere, but who will listen to me? I hope that out of ten thousand monks, one or two may pay attention to my words.

In India the skirt is worn crosswise round the body. The white cotton cloth of India is two cubits wide, and as it is only half the width required for making a skirt, it is difficult for a poor man to obtain a bigger piece. He has to join and sew together the two edges of the cloth and cut open the inside to meet his requirement. The rules for wearing garments are recorded in the Vinaya texts; I have only given a brief description of the essentials of the matter. No detailed explanation can be given unless we hold a face-to-face discussion.

216a Furthermore, all the garments of a homeless monk may be dyed in the color of *gandha* (myrrh), or of the yellow dust of glutinous *rehmannia,* vitex, philodendron, etc. These stuffs should be mixed with water in which red earth or red stone grains have been ground. One should make the color neither too deep nor too light, just to the point of meeting the requirement without taking too much trouble. Or one may just use the core of the sour jujube tree, or simply red earth and red stone grains, or birch leaf pear and earth-purple. As the color once dyed will last till the garment is worn out, why should one try to get any more kinds of dyestuffs? The bark of the mulberry tree and blue and green colors are prohibited, while true purple and brown colors are not used in the west.

As regards shoes and sandals, there are special instructions. Boots and thread-knitted shoes are completely banned as illegal. Embroidery and ornaments are not allowed by the Buddha, as is fully explained in the "Rules about Leather."

12. The Robes and Funeral Rites of a *Bhikṣuṇī*

In China the *bhikṣuṇī*s (Buddhist nuns) dress like laywomen, and their clothes are mostly contrary to the rules. According to the Vinaya, a *bhikṣuṇī* possesses five garments, namely, (1) the *saṃghāṭī,* (2) the *uttarāsaṅga,* (3) the *antarvāsa,* (4) the *saṃkakṣikā,* and (5) a skirt. The style of the first four garments is not dissimilar to those worn by a monk, but a nun's skirt is different. It is known as *kuśūlaka* in Sanskrit, meaning a silo-shaped skirt because it is sewn at both sides in the shape of a small silo. It is four cubits long and two cubits wide. It may cover up the navel and reach down to four fingers above the ankles. To wear the skirt, one steps into it, pulls it up to cover the navel, and then contracts the top of the skirt on both sides and ties it up with a double band in the back. The way of tying the band is more or less the same as that of monks.

Between the chest and the armpits [of a *bhikṣuṇī*], no breast cover should be tied. But if she is in her youth or in old age, when her breasts rise high or become flaccid, she may wear one without fault. Why should one put her to shame, saying that she does not know the rules and regulations? Free use of ornaments is blameworthy at the moment of putting them on or taking them off. At the time of death, she will have evil effects falling upon her like drizzling rain. If one has committed an offense only once out of many times, one should still make a timely repentance.

When going out, or in the presence of monks, or on being invited to accept a meal at a layman's house, a nun should put her *kāṣāya* round her neck to cover her body, and should not untie the strings at the shoulders. She should not expose her chest, and her hands should be thrust out from under her robe to take the food. A *saṃkakṣikā* which covers only one shoulder, and shirts and trousers, are prohibited by the Great Sage; they are unfit for a nun to wear.

In the countries of the South Seas, the nuns have a special garment. It is also called *saṃkakṣikā,* though not the same in style as in India. It is two cubits long and two cubits wide. The edges of it are sewn together, leaving about one foot not sewn in the center, and the upper corners are cut one inch open. To wear this garment, one holds it up, puts one's head and shoulders through the hole, and then pulls one's right shoulder out of it. It has no waistband; it covers one's sides, breasts, and navel; and it reaches below the knees. If one wishes to wear this garment, it is harmless to do so. It has only two fastenings, and is good enough to conceal shame. If one does not like to wear it, one may wear the *saṃkakṣikā*
216b worn by monks. In the chambers of a nunnery, it is adequate for a nun to wear only a *kuśūlaka* and a *saṃkakṣikā*. (Yijing's running note: I examined the Sanskrit texts and did not come across the name "shoulder-covering garment," which is actually the *saṃkakṣikā*. This is the original for the Chinese transliteration *qi-zhi*. It is not called a "skirt" in Chinese; perhaps the translators used different terms.) One should reject a garment which is against the rules and wear one which is made in compliance with the Buddha's teaching.

Making a *saṃkakṣikā* requires a full width and a half of silk or some cotton cloth four or five cubits in length. The way of wearing it is to put it over the shoulders in reverse, just as one wears the robe of five stripes. When going out to places other than one's chamber, one should be well covered. Even in the latrine, it is improper to leave the shoulders bare. In the spring and summer seasons one may use this garment to cover the body, while in the autumn and winter seasons, one may optionally put on warmer clothes.

By begging for food with an alms bowl, a nun may sufficiently maintain herself. Although she is a woman, she has the lofty aspirations of a man. Why should she always busy herself with the shuttle and loom and do miscellaneous work to make herself many garments, no less than five or ten? Some nuns never pay attention to meditation or the recitation of scriptures, being always driven by the vexations of an emotional temperament. They deck themselves with ornaments like laywomen, paying no regard to the texts on precepts. It befits all disciples to oversee and check on one another about their behavior.

In India none of the nuns act in such a way. All of them get their sustenance by begging for food and live a poor and simple life. But the nuns [in China] rarely have any beneficial support. The nunneries in which they abide are mostly devoid of a community supply of food, and if they did not try to earn a livelihood according to circumstances, they would have no way to keep themselves alive. If they do so, they are liable to act contrary to the teachings of the Vinaya and go against the Buddha's mind. Can they make a compromise and get out of the dilemma? It is said that when the body is at ease, the Way will flourish. But can we hear more about it in detail?

In reply I would say that one's original object in becoming homeless was to gain emancipation, so as to extirpate the noxious roots of the three trees [of greed, hatred, and stupidity] and to suppress the flood of the four torrents [of desire, continual existence, erroneous views, and ignorance]. One should follow the practice of austerity and keep off the wrong paths of suffering and enjoyment. One should strive hard to keep one's desires to a minimum, and pursue the true path of quietude. When one observes the precepts day and night, the Way will get on in the world. How can one think that it is reasonable to maintain the body in ease? If one can abide by the Vinaya rules and differentiate truth from falsehood, one will naturally be respected by dragons, spirits, and heavenly and human beings. Why should one worry about one's livelihood and toil without purpose? The five robes, a pot, and an alms bowl are enough for a nun to subsist upon, and a small cell is sufficient for her to live in. When one simplifies personal matters and spares one's disciples the trouble of attendance, one will be like a piece of jade lying undefiled in mire, or a pure lotus flower growing out of muddy water. Although such a nun may be a person of low rank, her wisdom is really equal to that of a superior personality.

Upon the death of their parents, [Chinese] monks and nuns perform rites and ceremonies unscrupulously, or they mourn over the dead as the bereaved children of a lay family would do, or arrange small mourning tables in their rooms to make offerings to the deceased, or wear a piece of dark-colored cloth in contradiction to regulations, or keep their hair long against the rules, or hold a wailing stick, or sleep on a straw mat in a mourning hut. All these practices are not taught by the Buddha, and they may well be omitted without committing a fault. What one should do, on account of the deceased, is to clean and decorate a room in which canopies and curtains may be temporarily fixed up for one to recite the scriptures and meditate on the Buddha while offering incense and flowers, so that the souls of the dead may be reborn in a
216c good place. This is the way for a filial offspring to requite the kindness of the deceased. Why should one live in mourning for three years to show off one's virtue, and fast for seven days as a way of repaying the kindness of one's dead parents? These actions will simply rebind the dead to earthly troubles to suffer more chains and fetters and pass from one dark place to another without knowing the twelve links of the chain of causality in the three divisions.

If one proceeds from death to death, how can one realize the ten stages of perfect achievement?

According to the teachings of the Buddha, when a *bhikṣu* is dead and his death has been ascertained, the corpse is carried to a crematorium on the same day and cremated soon afterwards. In the course of the cremation, his relatives and acquaintances gather together and sit at one side on bundles of straw, or on a heap of earth, or on bricks and stones. A competent monk is asked to recite from the *Anitya-sūtra,* a text on impermanence, as little as half a page or one page, so that it will not be tedious and tiresome. (Yijing's running note: This text has been copied and sent home separately.) Then all of them meditate on the impermanent nature of all things, and after that they return to their abodes. In a pond outside the monastery, they bathe themselves with their clothes on. If there is no pond, they may wash near a well. They wear old garments, so as not to spoil new ones. Then they change into dry clothes and return to their chambers. The ground is purified by the smearing of cow's dung, and all other things remain as usual. Not a bit of their dress is changed [for the occasion]. Sometimes *śarīra*s (ashes) are collected, and a stupa (a tumulus) is built. It is known as a *kūla* (a mound) and is in the shape of a small pagoda, but without the wheel sign on the top. The pagoda for an ordinary person and that for a Holy One are different, as is fully described in the Vinaya texts. How can we agree to discard the holy teachings of Śākyamuni, the Father, and pursue the secular burial rites taught by the Duke of Zhou, wailing for several months and wearing mourning apparel for three years? I heard that there was a Venerable Lingyu, who never performed a funeral service, nor did he put on mourning dress. In memory of the deceased, he cultivated meritorious deeds on their behalf. Some of the monks in the capital and at Luo-yang also followed his example. People may think that he was unfilial to behave so, but they do not know that his action was more in concordance with the gist of the Vinaya.

13. The Purification of a Site

There are five methods of purifying the ground of a site; namely, (1) purification through mental action, (2) purification through common consent, (3) a place resembling a cow lying down, (4) an old deserted place, and (5) purification through the assent of the assembly of monks.

Purification through mental action indicates that when the foundation stone has been laid for the construction of a monastery, the supervising *bhikṣu* should think thus, "At this spot in the monastery, or in the house, a pure kitchen should be built for the community of monks."

Common consent means that when the foundation stone of a monastery has been laid in the presence of, say, three monks, one of them should say to the other two, "Brethren, let us fix our attention to mark out this place in the monastery, or in the house, for the construction of a pure kitchen for the community of monks."
217a The second and the third monks should also repeat the same.

The place resembling a cow lying down means that the buildings of the monastery being erected are in the shape of a cow lying on the ground, with the doors of the chambers opened at random without a fixed plan. Even if no rites have been performed for its purification, such a place is considered pure by itself.

An old deserted place denotes a place which has long been abandoned and forsaken by the monks. If they come back, as soon as they reach the site, it is regarded as pure. But they cannot spend a night there unless a ceremony has been performed.

Purification through the assent of the assembly of monks means that approval of the boundaries of a site for building a monastery is given by the assembly of monks after due discussion of a proposal submitted to them for consideration. The details are related in the *Mūlasarvāstivāda-nikāya-ekaśata-karman*.

Once one of these five rites has been performed, the Buddha said, "This will enable all *bhikṣus* to have the double ability to cook food within and store it outside of the boundaries, or to cook food outside of and store it within the limits, both being without fault."

When I examined the rites of purification of the monks of the four schools, witnessed the actual practice at the present time, and made a careful study of the purport of the Vinaya, I found that the method of purification was roughly the same as what has been described above. If monks drink, eat, and lodge together at a place before it has been purified, they commit an offense of cooking and lodging [at an improper place]. Once it has been purified, they may drink, eat, and lodge together in the limits without committing the offense of cooking and lodging [at an improper place].

When we say a monastery, we imply that the whole monastic residence is a pure kitchen. In every chamber raw and cooked food may be stored. If a monk is not allowed to spend the night inside a monastery, can we drive him out to stay outside overnight? First, monks do not preserve berths for themselves, and secondly, keeping provisions in the monastery is permissible. It is the tradition of India to purify and demarcate the whole monastery as a kitchen, but to use a part of it as a kitchen is also permitted by the Vinaya. These views are not the same as those of the Vinaya masters in China.

If a monk stays away from the monastery for a night, without having purified and marked out a spot to keep his robes, he is blameworthy. If the spot has already been purified and marked out by the assembly of monks, he may leave his monastery to spend the night there without committing a fault. The same is the case with the pure kitchen. Since such is allowed by the Buddha, we must not stick to our own worldly opinions. The demarcation of a spot for safekeeping of one's robes is fixed in different ways, depending on whether it is under a tree or in some other place. It is just a boundary of protection, and is not meant to guard against women. If a [female] servant comes into the kitchen, shall we deem it a village? When one carries one's robes at the time of going to a village, it is not meant to guard oneself against women.

When the *karmadāna* (director of duties) goes round to supervise monastic affairs and carries his robes with him, it is really too burdensome for him.

14. The Summer Retreat of the Five Groups

The first summer retreat starts on the first day of the dark half of the fifth moon, and the second summer retreat begins on the first day of the dark half of the sixth moon. The summer retreat may be commenced only on these two days; no other date between them is fixed as the day to begin the retreat in the Vinaya texts. The first summer retreat concludes in the middle of the eighth moon, while the second terminates in the middle of the ninth moon. On the day when the retreat is drawing to its end, both monks and laymen perform a grand ceremony of alms-giving. The month after the middle of the eighth moon is called Kārttika (October-November). When a Kārttika congregation is held south of the Yangzi River in China, this is just the time to conclude the first
217b summer retreat. The sixteenth day of the eighth moon is the day to distribute the *kaṭhina* (inflexible) robes, or the robes of merit, as offerings to the monks. This is an ancient tradition.

It is said in a Vinaya text that during the summer retreat a monk may take leave with a good reason to go out of the monastery for one or more days as he is invited. If what he is doing can be done in one night, he must ask for permission for one day's absence, up to seven days for going in response to different invitations. If another occasion arises for him to go out, the Vinaya prescribes that he should apply for permission again. Should the absence exceed seven days, say eight days, or even up to forty nights, he should apply for permission from the general assembly of monks. Having received their unanimous permission, he may go out for eight or more days, but he should not stay out for half of the summer retreat. Thus leave is for forty nights at the most. When a sick person or some troublesome matter requires him to go out of the monastery to some other place, he may do so without being regarded as breaking the summer retreat, though he has not obtained permission beforehand.

When the five groups of the homeless disciples have settled down for the summer retreat, if a member of the lower grade has occasion for going out, he or she may ask another member to apply for permission in his or her stead. Before the commencement of the summer retreat, rooms are preassigned to the monks, the better rooms being allotted to the elder ones; thus all the rooms are distributed in order of seniority to the last person. Such rules are still practiced in Nālandā Monastery. The great assembly of monks assigns rooms every year; this is what the World-honored One has taught us to do with great benefit. Firstly, it may eliminate the concept of egoism, and secondly, the monastic rooms are generally looked after by all monks. All homeless monks should do so.

The monasteries south of the Yangzi River in China sometimes assign rooms to monks. This is a tradition handed down by the ancients, and it is still practiced at the present. How can one take a monastery as one's own property, just because one is living in it, without regarding whether such an action is permissible or not, till the end of one's life? It was because people of former generations did not observe the right conventions that men of subsequent ages lost sight of the Dharma. If the assignment of rooms is properly done according to the teachings of the Vinaya, it will give us great benefit.

15. The Ceremony of Confession

The last day of the summer retreat, which is also the end of the year, should be named *pravāraṇa* (the day one is free from restraint), when the monks are free to expose the misconduct of one another on the three bases [of having witnessed, having heard about, or having a suspicion of the misdeed], with the intention of absolving others from guilt. The word was formerly translated as *zi-zi* (self-release from restraint) according to its implication.

On the night of the fourteenth day, a teacher well versed in scriptures must be invited to mount a high seat to recite a Buddhist scripture, while lay devotees and monks gather together like clouds and mist, with lamps burning continually and incense and flowers offered. On the following morning, all of them go out round the village or town and worship the *caitya*s devoutly. They bring with them carriages with shelves and sedan chairs to carry images of the Buddha, while drums and other instruments sound under the sky, and banners and canopies, properly arranged, flutter high to shade out the sun. This is called the *sāmagrī,* translated as complete assemblage. All great festival days are celebrated in the same way as this. It is known in China as the procession going round the city.

When it is nearly noontime, they return to the monastery and have their regular meal at midday. In the afternoon, they gather together, each taking a handful of fresh cogon grass, and while
217c stamping their feet on it, they exercise their duty of free criticism. First come the monks and then the nuns, and lastly the three lower grades of the homeless disciples. If it is feared that owing to the large number of people attending the assembly, a long time might be required to complete the function, more members of the assembly should be appointed to hear the confessions. When one is accused of a fault, one should make a confession and ask for absolution according to usage.

At this time either the lay disciples offer gifts to the monks, or the monks exchange gifts among themselves. All alms received are brought into the presence of the assembly, and a confessor who possesses the five virtues [of being free from predilection, from anger, and from fear, of not being easily deceived, and of being able to discern shirkers of confession] should ask the presiding monk, "Can these alms be distributed to the members of the community of monks to be placed at their disposal?" The presiding monk says in answer, "Yes!" Then all robes, razors, needles, awls, and the like received from the donors are equally distributed to the monks. Such is the teaching of the Vinaya. The reason why razors and needles are offered to the monks on this day is that the donors wish them to acquire sharp intelligence and keen wisdom.

After the mutual criticism and the distribution of alms, the monks may disperse and each go his own way. This is the completion of the summer retreat, and there is no need for them to spend another night there. A full description is given elsewhere, and I shall not explain it here in detail.

The confession of guilt is to disclose one's own misdeeds and declare what offenses one has committed in the past, in order to rectify the past and prevent future faults with perfect sincerity and earnest self-reproach. The *poṣadha* (fasting) ceremony is conducted once every half month, and one should reflect every morning and evening on what offenses one has committed. (Yijing's running note: *Poṣa* means "nourishing," and *dha,* "purifying." Thus *poṣadha* means nourishing good deeds and purifying the guilt of violating the disciplinary rules. It was formerly transliterated as *pu-sha* in a wrongly abridged form.)

Committing any offense of the first group is irremediable, while violation of the rules of the second group requires a quorum of twenty members of the community of monks (to listen to the offender's confession and absolve him of his guilt). If one has committed a minor offense, one should make a confession to absolve one's fault before a monk who is not one's equal. Of the Sanskrit word *āpatti-pratideśanā, āpatti* means offense, and *pratideśanā,* confessing before others. It is in the hope of gaining purity that one confesses oneself guilty. One should confess of one's faults item by item, and then expiation may be expected. A general confession of faults is not allowed by the Vinaya. For confession we formerly said *chan-hui* in Chinese, which is actually irrelevant to the confession of misdeeds. Why? Because *kṣamā* (transliterated as *chan*) is an Indian word meaning "forbearance," while *hui* is a Chinese word meaning "repentance," and repentance has nothing to do with forbearance. If we strictly follow the Sanskrit text, we should say at the time of making confession,

"I confess my faults with a sincere mind." From this careful analysis, we may see that to translate *kṣamā* as repentance has scarcely any authority.

In India, when people, regardless of age, touched each other unintentionally or rubbed shoulders when passing each other, the senior one looked at the other person with his hands hanging down, while the junior one joined his hands palm to palm to pay due respect to the senior one, or to stroke his body or sometimes hold his shoulder, uttering the word "*Kṣamā,*" meaning "Please forgive me and do not be angry with me!" In the Vinaya the word *kṣamā* is used to express apology. Only when one confesses one's own faults is it known as *deśanā* (instruction). It is for fear of causing future misunderstanding that I have spoken about the errors introduced in former times. A habit may become a custom through long usage. However, we must follow the original regulations.

The Sanskrit word *pravāraṇa* is translated as optional. It also
218a means satisfying, indicating that one is free to disclose the faults of other monks at one's option.

16. The Use of Spoons and Chopsticks

In the west, the people use only the right hand for eating food, but a monk may be permitted to keep a spoon on account of illness. As regards chopsticks, they are not heard of in the five parts of India, nor are they mentioned in the Vinaya texts of the four schools of Buddhist monks. They are used only in China in the east. It is, of course, an old custom of the laypeople to use chopsticks, and monks may or may not use them according to their preference. The use of chopsticks is neither allowed nor disallowed, and this matter falls within the scope of the general rules of morality. If nobody derides or talks about the use of chopsticks, they may well be utilized in China. If a monk holds chopsticks [in India], the laypeople may sneer at him with contempt. But in India the people have never handled chopsticks. Such is the principle of the general rules of morality.

17. Salutation at Proper Times

The manner of paying homage should be in concordance with the rules; otherwise a prostration would merely be tumbling on the ground. Therefore, the Buddha said, "There are two kinds of impurity with which one should not receive salutation nor salute others." If one acts against this teaching, every bow one makes involves the fault of ill behavior.

What are the two kinds of impurity?

First, the impurity caused by eating and drinking. If one has eaten anything, even swallowed a tablet of medicine, one is unfit to receive salutation or salute others, unless one has rinsed one's mouth and washed one's hands. If one salutes others when one has not rinsed one's mouth and washed one's hands after having drunk juice or water, or even tea, honey, or other liquids, such as ghee, syrup, and the like, one commits a blunder as mentioned above.

Second, the impurity caused by going to the latrine. If one salutes others when one has not washed oneself clean and has not washed one's hands and rinsed one's mouth, or when one has not cleansed one's body or robes after they are defiled by excrement or soiled with mucus, saliva, etc., or when one has not chewed tooth wood in the morning, one commits a blunder as mentioned above. When the monks gather together to take a meal, one may just join one's hands palm to palm to show respect without paying a full salutation. If one pays a full salutation to others on such occasions, one is acting against the teaching. At a busy or narrow place, or at an unclean spot, if one salutes others, one also commits a similar blunder. All these points are described in the Vinaya texts. As the rules are handed down from a long time ago, and the [Chinese] monks are living in a cold country, it is rather difficult for them to behave in accordance with the teaching, even though they wish to do so. None of them does not find consolation in having fellow monks living under similar circumstances, and they would not care about minor offenses.

18. Answering the Call of Nature

I shall now give a brief account concerning evacuation. One should wear a bathing skirt on the lower part of the body, and put on a side-covering cloth for the upper part. One should then go to the latrine with a toilet jar filled with water, and close the door behind oneself to hide. Fourteen lumps of earth are prepared and placed on a piece of brick or stone, or on a small piece of board, outside the latrine. The size of the brick or board is one cubit long and half a cubit wide. The lumps of earth are ground into powder
218b and kept in separate heaps arranged in two rows. An additional lump is also placed there. One takes three balls of earth into the latrine and puts them aside. One of them is used for wiping the body and another one for washing it. The manner of washing the body is to first wash it with the left hand with water and then purify it with both water and earth. The remaining ball is used for roughly washing the left hand. If chips [of bamboo] are used [for cleaning purpose], they may be taken into the latrine, but they should be thrown out of the latrine after having been used. If some old paper must be used, it should be cast into the latrine after having been used. After having washed oneself clean, one may straighten one's garments with the right hand, put the jar aside, unfasten the door bolt with the right hand, and come out with the jar carried in the right hand. Or one may hold the jar in one's left arm with the left hand bending inwards, and close the door with the right hand before one leaves.

Then one comes to the place where the balls of earth are kept and squats down at one side. If one needs something to sit on, one may use anything one thinks fit at the time. The jar is placed on the left thigh and pressed down by the left arm. The seven balls of earth near oneself are used one by one to wash the left hand, and then the other seven are used one by one to wash both hands. The brick or board must be washed clean. The remaining ball is used for washing the jar, and then the arms, the thighs, and the feet, to make them all clean. After that one may go anywhere one wishes.

The water in the toilet jar is unfit for putting into the mouth or to the lips. After going back to one's chamber, one should rinse the mouth with water from a clean jar. In case one has touched the toilet jar after having finished the affair, one should again wash one's hands and rinse one's mouth; then one may touch other utensils. These are the rules, as roughly stated above, concerning relaxing the bowels. In order not to trouble others, a monk always washes himself, but it is not a fault to ask an attendant, if he has one, to wash for him. After urination, one or two balls of earth may be used for washing the hands and body. Purification is most important, as it is the foundation of veneration.

Some people may consider it a small matter, but the Vinaya severely berates [those who violate the rules]. If one has not washed oneself clean, one is unfit to sit on a seat of the monastery, nor should he worship the triple gem. By these rules Śāriputra once subdued the heretics. Thus the Buddha laid down the rules for monks in general. Those who practice these rules will gain the blessedness of observing the precepts of the Vinaya. If they do not, they go against the Buddha's teaching and will incur guilt. For a long time in the past, such rules were not introduced to China in the east.

Even if they had been introduced, they would have aroused the detestation [of the Chinese monks], who would have said: "In the Mahayana theory of complete voidness, what is pure and what is impure? Since the inside of the abdomen is full of filth, what is the use of washing the outside?" They do not know that by slighting and disparaging the teachings and disciplinary rules, they are slandering and calumniating the holy mind. They incur guilt either by receiving salutation or by paying salutation to others, and heavenly beings and spirits abhor their way of wearing robes and eating food. If a person does not wash himself clean, the people of all the five parts of India will laugh at him and he will be sneered at wherever he goes. Those who are engaged in propagating the Buddha's teachings should work for their dissemination. Since we 218c
have renounced worldly life and have relinquished our homes to

become homeless monks, we should abide by the words of Śākyamuni, the Father. Why should we cast angry stares at the sayings of the Vinaya texts? If one does not believe in these points, one had better try to follow the directives for washing oneself. After doing so for five or six days, one will grasp the defect of not washing oneself clean [after going to the latrine]. In the cold season, however, warm water must be prepared. In the three other seasons, one may use whatever water one likes. But the use of a water tube or a trough and a piece of silk for wiping is not based on the Vinaya texts. There are some people who keep some water in their mouth and leave the latrine, and this is also against the rules of purification.

For a monastery there must be, first of all, a latrine built and kept clean. If the monks are unable to make one, they may instruct some devotees to build one for the use of all monks, whether holy or ordinary ones, coming from the ten quarters. It is important not to spend much money for it. Such is the way of purification, which is by no means a futile action.

A big trough capable of holding one or two *shi* (one *shi* equals one hundred liters), filled with earth, should be prepared and put beside the latrine, as the monks have no place to store earth in their private chambers. If a monk does not actually possess a water jar, he is allowed to use a porcelain or earthen pot to carry water and put it aside in the latrine. He may use his right hand to wash himself harmlessly.

In the regions of the Yangzi and Huai Rivers, many latrines are made of big earthen urns half buried below the surface of the ground. One should not wash oneself at such places. Separate washing places should be prepared, preferably at spots with streams of flowing water. In such monasteries as Bao-fu Monastery at Fen-zhou, Ling-yan Monastery at Mount Dai, Yu-quan Monastery in the capital city of Jing-zhou, and the White Pagoda Monastery at Yang-zhou, the latrines are built quite in accordance with the traditional rules, except for the lack of a supply of water and earth. Had some people taught them the proper way of doing it, the arrangement would have been the same as that at Rājagṛha. This is due to the indifference of the former sages; the pupils of late times are not to be blamed for being ignorant.

The earth as well as the water stored in a jar that is kept in the latrine should be safely placed and sufficiently supplied; there should be no shortages. It is better to use a water pot with a spout to replenish the jar. If one wishes to keep a bottle, the rules for that have been related before. A copper bottle with a lid over the wide mouth is unsuitable for washing. But if a hole is made in the side of the bottle, the top is welded with tin, and a small aperture is made in the protruding point on the top, it may also be used as a makeshift to meet the requirements of the time.

Supplemental Remarks

I have toiled with my pen and paper to express my deep and earnest sentiments, with the hope that some people will accept my remonstrances as water follows the course of a stream. The Great Sage has passed into the state of calm between the twin *śāla* trees, and the arhats have become ashes in the five parts of India. The Dharma they have left behind is still exerting influence up to this morning. We should follow the example of those who have given up their lives and draw our inspiration from the ones who have abandoned the world. We should forsake the troubles that cause turbidity in our minds, and should admire the brilliant world of purity. Let both external defilements and internal delusions be cleared away, and the upper ties together with the lower bondages be completely destroyed. Our traces in life will be inactive and our spirits will become clear and bright. In any one of the four postures [of walking, standing, sitting, and lying], we shall cause no involvement, and the three honored ones [the Buddha, the Dharma, and the Sangha] will be near and dear to us. Since we
are not mocked by living people, why should we fear the anger of 219a
the lord of death? With my thoughts concentrated on benefiting

all sentient beings of the nine happy states, I shall complete the good cause of realizing Buddhahood in three long ages. I sincerely hope that one man out of ten thousand rectifies himself through my words. Then I shall not regret the pains and hardships I have suffered during the last twenty years and more.

End of Fascicle Two

Fascicle Three

19. Regulations for Ordination

The rules for becoming a monk in the western country of India were all laid down by the Holy One, and are extensively related in the *Mūlasarvāstivāda-nikāya-ekaśata-karman*. Here I shall just sketch them in brief. Anyone who has the intention of becoming a homeless monk may go of his own free will to a teacher whom he likes and inform him of his wish. The teacher then makes in an expedient way the necessary inquiries as to whether the applicant [has committed] patricide or matricide, etc. After having found that he has committed none of the serious crimes that would bar him from entering the community of monks, the teacher agrees to accept him. Having been accepted, the applicant is permitted to relax and rest for ten days up to one month. Then the teacher imparts to him the five precepts, whereupon he is named an *upāsaka* (a male lay devotee). Before that he is not counted among the seven groups of Buddhist disciples; this is the basic step for entering the teachings of the Buddha. The teacher then prepares for him a stripeless robe, a *saṃkakṣikā,* and an undergarment, as well as an alms bowl and a strainer, before he makes a statement to the assembly of monks, informing them that a candidate wishes to become a monk. With the consent of the assembly of monks, the teacher, on behalf of the candidate, asks a monk to be the candidate's *ācārya* (instructor). At a secluded place a barber shaves his hair and beard, and cold or warm water is prepared according to the season for him to take a bath. After that the teacher helps him to put on the undergarment and conveniently ascertains that he is not a eunuch, etc. Then the teacher gives him the outer garment, which he receives by putting it over his head. Having put

on the religious robe, the candidate is given the alms bowl. This is known as the ceremony of home-leaving. Next, in the presence of the teacher, the *ācārya* imparts the ten precepts to the candidate,
219b either by reciting them or reading from a text. After having received the ten precepts, he is known as a *śrāmaṇera* (novice). (Yijing's running note: This is translated as "seeker of quietude," meaning he who aims to seek the condition of perfect quietude of nirvana. The old transliteration was *sha-mi,* which is too short and the pronunciation is incorrect. It was translated as one who has entered the life of rest and shows loving kindness to all. The meaning is accurate, but without authority.)

The regulations, the disciplinary rules, the asking for instruction, and the solicitation of permission from the Sangha are the same in substance for all qualified candidates who proceed to receive ordination. According to the Vinaya texts, a *śrāmaṇera* is not considered guilty if he has committed any of the twelve particular offenses, but for a *śikṣamāṇā* (probationary female novice) there are some modifications of the rules. What are the twelve offenses?

1. Failure to distinguish between (legal and illegal) robes.
2. Sleeping without wearing a garment.
3. Touching fire.
4. Eating to excess.
5. Injuring living things.
6. Discarding filth upon green grass.
7. Climbing up a tall tree without purpose.
8. Touching jewels.
9. Eating leftover food.
10. Digging in the ground.
11. Refusing to accept offerings of food.
12. Damaging growing sprouts.

For the two lower grades of members of the Sangha (male and female novices), the commission of these twelve offenses does not incur guilt, but for the *śikṣamāṇā*s the nonobservance of the last five rules incurs guilt. All of these three lower-grade members should observe the summer retreat. The six major rules and six auxiliary ones (for *śikṣamāṇās*) are spoken of elsewhere. If they can observe these rules, they may be considered in concordance with the Dharma and counted among the five groups of Buddhist disciples, being worthy to receive the material advantages offered to them. How can a teacher not impart the ten precepts to one who has left home to become a monk, out of fear that he might break them, and thus he could not receive full ordination? In such a case the novice would merely bear the false name of being a *śrāmaṇera* and vainly assume the title of a monk. He seems to have enjoyed a small advantage, but actually he suffers a great loss. It is said in a scripture, "One who has not received the ten precepts, though counted as a member of the Sangha, has a seat only temporarily, and how can he hold it for long?"

In the Divine Land of China one becomes a monk and leaves his home by public registration. After shaving his hair with government permission, he goes to live with a teacher for some time. The teacher does not take care to make any of the inquiries of the disciple, nor does the disciple request the impartation of the ten precepts. Before receiving full ordination, such a person commits all sorts of guilty actions unscrupulously. On the day of receiving full ordination, he is simply led to the altar without previous knowledge of the rites laid down in the Vinaya. How can he behave properly at the time of the ceremony? This is not right for maintaining the Way. He is neither fit to be a resident monk of a monastery, nor is there any doubt about the debt he incurs by receiving the alms given to him. He should act according to the teachings for the salvation of himself and others.

One who becomes a monk by permission of the government should ask a monk beforehand to be his teacher, who will first make the inquiries and then, if he is found pure of the impedimental crimes, teach him the five precepts. After seeing him having his hair shaved, the teacher then dresses him in a stripeless robe and imparts to him the ten precepts.

When the novice has become acquainted with the religious rites, has reached the required age, and wishes to receive full ordination, the teacher, having seen that the disciple is capable of keeping the disciplinary rules with resolution, may prepare the six requisites for him and invite nine other monks [to be witnesses]. The ceremony may be legitimately performed on a small terrace, in a large enclosure, or within a natural boundary. Inside the limited area for the function, mats belonging to the Sangha may be used or each monk may bring his own mat for a seat. Some incense and flowers may be prepared in an inexpensive way. The candidate is taught to pay respect three times to each of the monks, or sometimes to approach each of them and touch his feet as a sign of homage. Both ways are proper manners of salutation taught by the Buddha.

219c After having paid homage to the monks, the candidate is instructed to beg for full ordination. When he has done so three times, his teacher gives him the robes and an alms bowl in the presence of the monks assembled for the occasion. The bowl should be carried around and be shown to each of the monks. If it is proper in mode, all of them should say, "A good bowl!" If they did not say anything, they would incur the fault of infringing the Dharma. After that the ceremony of ordination is conducted according to the Dharma. The *karmācārya* (chief ceremony officiant) holds a text and reads it aloud, or recites it from memory, both being allowed by the Buddha. The one who has received the disciplinary rules is known as an *upasaṃpanna*. (Yijing's running note: *Upa* means "near to" and *saṃpanna,* "completeness," indicating nirvana. Having received full ordination, one is near to nirvana. The old translation is "fullness," which gives a general idea of the term.) As soon as the ceremony is completed, one should immediately measure the shadow of the sun and note down distinctly the name of one of the five seasons.

The shadow of the sun is measured in the following manner. Take a fine stick, about the size of a slender chopstick one cubit long. Bend it at a point four finger-widths from one end and make it into the shape of a carpenter's square, but mind that the shorter part of the stick is not broken away from the longer section. Let the shorter part stand erect under the sun, and place the longer section on the ground, overlaying the shadow cast by the shorter part of the stick. Then measure the shadow with four fingers. A length of fully four finger-widths is called one *puruṣa*. Thus we have so many *puruṣa*s of time, or sometimes one *puruṣa* and one finger-width or half a finger-width, or simply one finger-width of time, etc. In this way time is measured and calculated by adding or reducing the number of finger-widths. (Yijing's running note: The word *puruṣa* is translated as "man." The length of four finger-widths of shadow is called one *puruṣa,* because when the shadow of the vertical stick, which is four finger-widths long, casts a shadow of the same length on the ground, the shadow of a man standing under the sun will measure the same as his height. When the shadow of the vertical stick is eight finger-widths long, the man's shadow on the ground is double his height. Such is the case with a man of medium height; it is not necessarily so with all persons. Other measurements of time are also made by the same method.) But it must be made clear whether it is before or after the [midday] meal. When the weather is cloudy or at night, the measurement should be made in an appropriate way as one thinks fit.

According to the method adopted in China, we put a ruler vertically under the sun at midday to measure the shadow of the sun, or to mark the twelve two-hour periods of a day and night. The five seasons are counted in various ways in different regions, and the number of months in the year is sometimes odd and sometimes even. Thus it is difficult to know them with certainty, unless they are explained with reference to a specific matter.

The first season is winter, which consists of four months, from the sixteenth day of the ninth moon to the fifteenth day of the first moon. The second season is spring, which also consists of four months, from the sixteenth day of the first moon to the fifteenth day of the fifth moon. The third one is the rainy season, which lasts only one month, from the sixteenth day of the fifth moon to the fifteenth day of the sixth moon. The fourth one is the final season, which lasts only one day and night on the sixteenth day of the sixth moon. The fifth one is the long season, which lasts from the seventeenth day of the sixth moon to the fifteenth day of the ninth moon. This system laid down by the Buddha for dividing the seasons is found only in the Vinaya texts, and there is evidently a deep significance in it. According to the usages of different localities, the year is divided into three, four, or six seasons, as is mentioned elsewhere.

In India or on the islands of the South Seas, when one monk meets another one for the first time, he asks the other one, "Venerable One, how many times have you done the summer retreat?" The other one answers, "So and so many times." If they have done the same number of summer retreats after ordination, the inquirer asks the other one in which season he was ordained. If they were ordained in the same season, the inquirer again asks the number of days left in that season when he was ordained. If
220a the number of days left in that season is also the same, the one asks the other whether he was ordained before or after the meal on that day. In case both of them were ordained in the forenoon, then they inquire about the length of the shadow under the sun at the moment of ordination. If there is any difference in the length of the shadow, the seniority of the two is determined. If there is no difference, the two of them are of equal standing. In that case, the order of seats is arranged according to the principle of priority of arrival, and the duty-distributor may allow either of them to take precedence over the other in performing religious duties.

Those who go to India must be acquainted with these points. It is unlike in China, where the monks just inquire about the date of ordination. But in Nālandā Monastery the monks often receive full ordination when the [first] morning of the long season has just dawned. They mean to claim seniority over most of the monks ordained in the same summer. It corresponds with the dawn of the seventeenth day of the sixth moon in China. They do not want the ordination to fall on the date of commencement of the second summer retreat. (Yijing's running note: This is according to the method of observing the summer retreat in India. If we follow the old practice in China, the date would fall on the seventeenth day of the fifth moon.) One who receives ordination when the night is drawing to the end on the sixteenth day of the sixth moon is the most junior monk among all monks ordained in the same summer because he is ordained in the second summer retreat.

After having received ordination, the disciple does not have to make offerings to others, but if his teacher has the means, he may prepare on behalf of his disciple some gifts, such as a girdle, a strainer, and the like, for the monks whose presence is required for the performance of the ceremony at the altar of ordination, in order to express his mind of gratitude. Then the *upādhyāya* (spiritual teacher) gives the *Text of the Disciplinary Rules* to the disciple and teaches him the character of offenses and how to recite the rules. When the disciple is well learned in the rules, he will read the full text of the *Vinaya-piṭaka* (*Collection of Books on Monastic Discipline*), which he recites every day and tries to observe from morning to morning. If he does not live up to them constantly, he might lose his mental power. When he has studied the *Vinaya-piṭaka,* he begins to learn the sutras and *śāstra*s. Such is the way a teacher instructs his disciple in India. Although a long period has passed since the time of the Sage, this method of instruction still prevails unaltered. Therefore, these two teachers are likened to one's parents. Is it right for a monk to undergo unusual toil and fatigue because of a desire to receive ordination, yet pay no heed to the disciplinary rules when he has been taught to observe them? It is a pity that one should have started a good cause, but failed to carry it through to the end!

There are some people who desire to be ordained at the moment when they first meet their teachers, but once they are ordained, they come to study under their teachers no more. They neither read the book on the precepts nor do they open the texts of the Vinaya, but unworthily enjoy the advantages of being among the ranks of monks, doing harm to themselves as well as to others. Such people will cause the downfall of the Dharma.

According to the practice of India, after a monk has received full ordination, he is called a *dahara* (junior monk), which is translated into Chinese as "small teacher." When he has passed ten full summer retreats, he is known as a *sthavira* (an elder), which is translated as "abiding position." As a monk of ten years' standing he is in a position to leave his teacher and abide by himself. He may also act as an *upādhyāya* (officiant at the ceremony of ordination).

In writing letters or exchanging communications, a monk should style himself Śramaṇera so-and-so, or Dahara Bhikṣu so-and-so, or Sthavira Bhikṣu so-and-so, as the case may be. If he is well versed in both Buddhist learning and worldly lore and is a man of high virtue and noble character, he may call himself Bahuśruta (well-learned) Bhikṣu so-and-so. But one must not designate oneself Sangha so-and-so, because the term Sangha means a group of no less than four persons. How can one individual use an appellation indicating a group of persons to denote one man? In India there is no such custom as calling oneself a Sangha.

One who becomes an *upādhyāya* must be a *sthavira,* having passed ten full summer retreats. There is no seniority requirement for the *karmācārya* who acts as a private tutor and the other monks who serve as witnesses, but they must be well learned in the Vinaya and pure in observing all the disciplinary
220b rules. It is said in the Vinaya that to call one an *upādhyāya* who is not an *upādhyāya,* or to call one an *ācārya* who is not an *ācārya,* or vice versa, defiling the name of *upādhyāya,* incurs the guilt of evil-doing. If a man inquires, "What is the name of your *upādhyāya?*" or "Whose disciple are you?", or when one is obliged to mention the name of one's teacher, one should say, "In the circumstances, I am obliged to tell the name of my *upādhyāya,* whose name is so-and-so." In India and on the islands of the South Seas, it is not haughty to use the word "I." It is also not a rude form of address if one says "you." It is simply meant to distinguish one person from another, without a mind of contempt towards others. This is not like in China, where it is considered

despicable to use such pronouns. If one dislikes using the word "I," one may say "this person" instead of "I." These points were taught by the Buddha, and it is fitting to put them into practice. One should not echo what others have said, making no distinction between right and wrong.

When laymen who are dressed in white come to the residence of *bhikṣu*s to study Buddhist texts exclusively, with the intention of shaving their hair and becoming monks clad in black robes, they are called "children of men." Those who come to seek secular learning without the mind to relinquish the world are known as "students." These two classes of pupils have to provide food for themselves. (Yijing's running note: In the monasteries of India there are in most cases students who have come to learn secular literature from the *bhikṣu*s. They may serve, on the one hand, as attendants to their teachers, and, on the other hand, they may cherish pious aspirations because of the instructions imparted to them. As this is beneficial to both sides, there is no harm in keeping these students. Each of them should keep only one alms bowl like an ascetic, so as not to cause any trouble to others. But if fractional alms are given to them, it is also permitted. Let them distribute tooth wood to the monks and serve at meals. To supply them with sufficient timely requirements is not detrimental to the principle of compassion.) To let them partake of the food of the permanent Sangha is totally banned by the holy teachings. But if they have done some hard work for the community, they may be given either ordinary food or food purposely prepared for them beforehand by donors, which they may take without committing a misdeed.

The brilliance [issuing from the Buddha] at the Nairañjanā River has faded away, and his radiance on Vulture Peak has disappeared. How many arhats have survived to transmit the Dharma? Thus it is said in a *śāstra:* "Since the Great Teacher closed his eyes, those who have realized sainthood have also passed away one after another. In this time when moral defilements are on the increase, we should be more diligent and never relax our spiritual efforts." All the virtuous monks should work together to safeguard the Dharma. If we are listless and inert and give the reins to self-conceit, whither shall we guide men and heavenly beings? It is said in the Vinaya: "So long as the disciplinary rules are observed, my Dharma will not perish. If there is no one observing the rules, my Dharma will come to an end." It is also said: "When the precepts exist, I exist." These are not empty words; they imply a deep meaning and are truly worthy of our respect.

Let me repeat it:

The shadow of the Great Teacher has faded,
With it the Dharma will perish.
Lofty is the mountain of heresy,
The hill of wisdom has collapsed.
The reillumination of the sun of Buddha
Depends upon men of good virtue.
If we follow the small path,
Who will propagate the great Way?
Let us pray that the well-learned masters
Do their best to bring about its spread.
We hope the Way will thrive without fail,
220c Passing through endless ages with good fame.
Where rests the good fame?
In the active waves in the sea of precepts.
Thus the teaching will not perish, though near the end.
Actions will not go astray, even on the verge of error.
This coincides with the right words spoken at Rājagṛha.
One's deeds will not break the rules of the Jeta Grove.

20. The Times for Taking a Bath

The customs regarding taking baths in India are different from those in China. In India the climate is temperate with slight variations in different regions. There are flowers and fruits throughout the year, even in the twelfth month. Snow and ice are unknown, except for a thin layer of frost. Although the weather is hot at most times, the heat is never unbearable. Even in hot weather, people do not suffer from prickly heat, and in the cold season, their feet are not chapped. Because of this [moderate climate], the people take baths frequently and set store by bodily cleanliness. Every day they do not eat before having washed themselves. There are ponds full of water in all places, and the people consider it a meritorious deed to dig ponds. If we travel from one post house to another, we may come within sight of twenty or thirty bathing ponds along the way, which measure one to five *mu* (one *mu* equals one-fifteenth hectare) in size. On all four sides of the ponds, there are planted *tāla* trees (palmyra trees) growing to a height of forty or fifty feet. Rainwater is collected in the ponds, which are as limpid as a clear river. At the eight *caitya*s, there are the ponds in which the World-honored One bathed himself. The water in these ponds is so clear and serene that it looks different from that in other ponds.

At Nālandā Monastery there are more than ten large bathing pools, and every morning an instrument is sounded to call the monks to take baths. Every one of them brings his bathing skirt, and hundreds or thousands of monks go out of the monastery in all directions to the pools to bathe themselves. The bathing skirt is worn in the following manner. Take a piece of soft cotton cloth five forearms in length and one and a half forearms wide. Wrap it round the body, and then draw off the undergarment beneath it. Both ends of the bathing skirt are pulled to the front. Then take hold of the upper corner of the left end with the right hand and stretch it down to the waist to touch the body. The right end is twisted with the left one, and both are pressed in between the waist and the skirt itself. This is the way of wearing a bathing skirt. The skirt worn at bedtime is also put on in the same way.

At the time of coming out of the bathing pool, one should shake one's body and emerge from the water slowly, for fear that some insects may cling to the skirt and be taken out of the water. How to come up to the bank is described in detail in the Vinaya texts. If a monk does not go to a bathing pond but takes a bath in the monastery, the bathing skirt is also put on in the same way, and someone is asked to pour the water for him. A screen may be put up anywhere at any time.

The World-honored One taught us how to build a bathroom, or construct an open-air pool with bricks, or make a medical bath for the treatment of disease. He also taught us to anoint the whole body, rub the feet with ointment every night, and dab the head with oil every morning. Doing so is very good for keeping clear eyesight and warding off the cold.

Furthermore, one should take a bath before eating food. There are two benefits derived from eating food after taking a bath. First, the body is pure and empty, without any dirt. Second, one will have a good appetite, as one's phlegm and mental depression are dissolved after taking a bath. Bathing after taking a square meal
221a is forbidden by the science of medicine. Thus we may know that the saying about "washing one's hair when one is hungry and taking a bath with a full stomach" is not the opinion of an all-round scholar. Using a bathing wrapper three feet long, too short to cover the body, or taking a bath naked without wearing anything, is incongruous with the teachings of the Buddha. One should use a bathing skirt four times as long as it is wide, big enough to cover the body in a decent manner. This is not only compatible with the holy teachings, but also causes no shame in the presence of men and heavenly beings. One should also know about other things that are unwise. Even when taking a bath at night, one should not be unbecoming in appearance. How can one uncover oneself before people's eyes?

21. The Cloth for Sitting On

To spread the sitting cloth [or mat] on the ground for worshiping is not the practice in the five parts of India. Nor is it mentioned in the rules of the four schools that one should crouch down and stand up three times in salutation. How worshipers pay homage will be described in other chapters.

To make a cloth for sitting, a piece of cloth is cut [in two], one part being placed upon the other and stitched together. There is no time for me to give a full description of its measurement. The cloth is needed to preserve the mattresses of others when one intends to sleep thereon. In case one has to use anything belonging to others, whether old or new, one must cover it with one's own sitting cloth. If it is one's own property and is old, one need not cover it with the sitting cloth. One must not soil or spoil the gifts presented by donors.

The sitting cloth is not used for worshiping. The monks [of the islands] in the South Seas keep a cotton kerchief, three or five feet long and folded like a napkin, which they place under their knees as a pad when paying homage. When they are walking, they carry it on their shoulders. All *bhikṣus* coming from India smiled at them [because of their curious custom].

22. Rules Concerning Sleeping and Resting

In India, as the living quarters [of the monks] are narrow and limited, where there are many residents, the beds are lifted up after the monks have arisen [in the morning]. The beds are put together at one side of the rooms, or removed and stored away out of doors. A bed is two cubits (one cubit equals eighteen to twenty-two inches) broad and four and a half cubits long, with a mattress and a mat of the same size, both of which are light and not heavy. The ground is then wiped clean with dry cow dung, and sitting couches, blocks of wood, small mats, etc., are arranged. The monks take their seats in accordance with their seniority and perform their usual duties. All the utensils for their sustenance are placed on shelves. There is no rule that the bed must be screened with a piece of robe. If one is not qualified to sleep in the monks' quarters, one should not do so, and if one is qualified to sleep there, why should one hide oneself behind a robe screen?

Before using a bed belonging to the Sangha (community of monks), one must put a covering on it first. The sitting cloth is suitable for this purpose. If one does not do so, one is apt to suffer the grief of having a black back. This was taught by the Buddha, and one must not be negligent about it.

In the ten islands of the South Seas, as well as in the five parts of India, people do not use wooden pillows to support the head. This is a custom prevalent only in China. The pillows used in India
221b are all similar in style. Silk or cotton, dyed in any color according to one's liking, is sewn into a straight bag, one and a half cubits long and half a cubit wide. It is stuffed with material produced everywhere, such as wool, hemp fiber, cattail pollen, willow catkins, kapok, reed catkins, vines of the great trumpet flower, soft leaves, dry moss, *cassia tora,* ramie, or spotted peas. It may be high or low according to whether the season is cold or hot, just to make it comfortable and restful for the body, without feeling hard or stiff. But a wooden pillow is rough and strong, and as wind may pass below the neck, it often causes headaches. Customs, however, differ in various lands, and different things are appreciated. I am just narrating here what unusual things I have heard, and it is up to the reader to decide what customs he should adopt. But things of a warm nature tend to keep off cold, and ramie and peas are good for brightening eyesight. All these things are beneficial and may be used without fault. If one exposes the head to cold in a chilly country, one is liable to suffer from febrile diseases, and catarrh in the winter season is also due to the same cause. If one keeps the head warm properly, one may be free from such diseases. The saying "keep the head cold but keep the feet warm" is not always trustworthy.

A holy image [of the Buddha] is sometimes placed in a monk's room, either on a windowsill or in a niche specially made for it. When sitting down to take a meal, the monks screen off the image with a cloth curtain. They bathe it every morning and offer incense and flowers to it regularly. Every day at noon, the monks offer food to it when taking a meal. The case for storing scriptures is placed at one side. At sleeping time they stay in a separate room. In the various islands of the South Seas, the custom is the same. Such is the way the monks venerate the Buddha at ordinary times in their private rooms. The holy images of a monastery are all installed in a special shrine hall. How can an image, after having been made, never be washed and wiped during its lifetime? If it is not a festival day, why should one offer food frequently to an image? To speak from this point of view, what is the harm in living in the same room with an image [of the Buddha]? When the Great Teacher was living, he permitted the monks to live in the same room with him. An image is but a representation of the real person. Logically speaking, there is no harm in doing so. This is a long-standing tradition practiced in India.

23. Walking Up and Down for Good Health

In the five parts of India, both monks and laymen are in the habit of taking a walk, going straight forward and coming back along the same route at proper times when they feel like it, but they do not take walks in noisy places. First, it cures diseases, and second, it helps digestion. When noontime is approaching, or when the sun is to the west, it is time to take a walk. They may either go out of the monastery for a long walk, or just stroll slowly in the corridor. If one does not do so, one is liable to suffer from illness, being often troubled by swelling of the legs and of the stomach, or pain in the elbows or in the shoulders, or with phlegmatic symptoms which will not dissolve. All these ailments are caused by our sedentary posture. If one can take this exercise, one will have a healthy body and increase one's spiritual cultivation.

So there are paths on which the World-honored One used to take walks at Vulture Peak, under the bodhi tree, at Deer Park, in the city of Rājagṛha, and at other holy sites. They are about two cubits wide, fourteen or fifteen cubits long, two cubits high, 221c
and built with bricks. On the surface [of each of the paths], there are

fourteen or fifteen limestone sculptures of blooming lotus flowers about two cubits high and one foot in diameter, symbolizing the footprints of the Holy One. At both ends of the paths, there are small *caitya*s, equal to a man's height, in which standing statues of Śākyamuni are sometimes installed. One goes round a *caitya* just as one goes round a temple, with one's right shoulder towards the venerated object. As this is a special meritorious deed, one should perform it with piety and respect.

Taking a walk for exercise is a way to stimulate digestion and relieve boredom. It is meant to preserve good health or to cure illness. It was formerly known as *xing-dao* (walking along the Way) or as *jing-xing* (taking a walk), both of which have the same meaning, without any difference. But this health-preserving exercise has been lacking in China for a long time. It is said in a scripture, "They walked while looking at the trees." I have seen the path used [by the Buddha] for taking walks beside the Diamond Seat, but I did not see any of the round pedestals.

24. The Junior Worshiping the Senior

The rites of salutation should be practiced according to the Buddha's teachings. A monk whose seniority is determined by the measurement of a shadow [with a sundial] at the time of receiving full ordination is entitled to be saluted by his juniors. The Buddha said, "There are two kinds of men who are worthy to be saluted. First, the Tathāgata (one who has attained Buddhahood), and second, senior *bhikṣu*s." Since this is the golden word of the Buddha, why should we take the trouble to be humble and timorous? When a junior monk sees a senior one, he should express respect in a polite manner, uttering the word "*Vande*" ("I salute") while he worships the senior monk. When a senior monk is worshiped by a junior one, he may just sit up straight with his hands in front and say "*Ārogya*" ("May you be healthy!"). (Yijing's running note: This is a form of blessing, meaning "May you be free from illness.") If they do not say these words, both of them are at fault. [The one who is saluted] may remain standing or sitting as he is, without changing his posture. Since he is entitled to receive salutation, he need not salute in return. Such is the rule for the monks of the five parts of India.

How can a junior monk expect a senior one to stand up when the salutation is about to take place? Nor should the senior monk, while receiving salutation, fear that he might displease or annoy the junior one. If so, the honored one would get hold of the junior monk to prevent him from paying homage, while saying, "Don't take the trouble!" Thus the junior monk would try hard to salute the senior one, but he could not reach the ground [to prostrate himself]. If they did not behave so, they would be criticized as acting against etiquette! Alas! They disregard the holy teachings to satisfy their human feelings. Both the one who is paying respect and the one who is respected are acting against the rules. We should make a deep study of this point. A long stream has been overflowing for a long time, and who would try to bring it under control with a dam?

25. Behavior between Teacher and Pupil

The instruction of pupils is an important factor for the prosperity [of the Dharma]. If we do not pay attention to it, the extinction of the Dharma may be expected. We must take precautionary measures about the matter, and must not let it slip off [as a fish slips off] the net.

It is said in the Vinaya: "Early every morning, a pupil should first chew tooth wood, and then come to his teacher to offer him tooth wood, gleditsia [used for soap], water, and a towel, which are put at the sitting place. When these things are properly arranged, he goes to worship the holy image of the Buddha, walks round the shrine hall, and then returns to his teacher's place, where he, having tidied up his robe, makes a salutation without standing up. Putting his palms together, he touches the ground with his head three times, and while kneeling on the ground with his 222a head bowed down and his hands joined together, he inquires of his teacher, 'May my *upādhyāya* be attentive!'" (Yijing's running note: *Upa* means "near to," and *adhyāya*, "a teacher." In India well-learned people are generally called *wu-she,* which is not a classical term [but a corrupt abbreviation]. According to Sanskrit scriptures and disciplinary texts, the word *upādhyāya,* meaning a personal teacher, is used. In the various northern countries, the word is pronounced as *he-she,* and the translators adopted it [to indicate a monk] erroneously.) Or the pupil may say, "May my *ācārya* be attentive!" (Yijing's running note: *Ācārya* is translated as "instructor." He is competent to instruct the pupil in religious rites. Formerly it was mistransliterated as *a-she-li.*) "Now I beg to inquire whether the *upādhyāya* has slept well last night, whether his four elements [of the physical body] are in peace and harmony, whether he is easy and agile in movement and has a good digestion, and whether he is ready to take his morning meal." These inquiries may be lengthy or brief according to circumstances.

The teacher answers the inquiries according to whether he is at ease or not, as the case may be. Then the pupil goes to the adjoining rooms to salute his seniors. Next, he reads a short section of a scripture and memorizes what he has learned before. He studies new lessons every day and reviews his old acquirements each month, without wasting a single moment. He should wait after daybreak, and then ask permission of his teacher to take the morning meal, if he has a good appetite for it. He need not take the trouble to seek porridge before dawn, in such haste as not to ask permission of his teacher, without chewing tooth wood, nor having time to ascertain that the water [for his daily use] is free from insects, and even without having washed and cleansed himself. Does he not know that for the sake of one bowl of porridge, he is acting against the four points of the Buddha's teaching? The causes of errors and degeneracies come from this violation. I wish that those who maintain and support the Dharma will consider the matter well. (Yijing's running note: The above-mentioned inquiries are according to the rules taught in Āryadeśa [the holy land], *ārya* meaning "holy," and *deśa,* "land," that is, the western country of India. Saints and sages emerged there one after another, hence the name commonly used by the people. It is also known as Madhyadeśa [the Midland Country], as it is in the middle of millions of countries. Owing to this fact, the name is known to all. In the countries of the Hu tribes of the north, the holy land is only known as Xi-du [Sindhu], which is not a popular name, but a dialectical appellation without any special meaning. When this name is heard in India, most people do not know where it is, and so it is fitting to call India the Holy Land, which is a suitable name. Or, it is said by tradition that the word Indu is translated as "moon," which is correct, but it is not a popular designation. It is just like the Land of Great Tang being known in India as Cīna, which is simply a name without special meaning. Furthermore, we should know that the five parts of India are collectively known as the Brahmanic Country, while the country of Suri in the north is included in the territory of the Hu tribes. They should not be mixed up and called by one and the same name.)

When one has received full ordination, after having shaved one's hair and put on the plain robe of a homeless monk, one has to ask permission of one's teacher to do anything, with the exception, according to the Vinaya, of five things; otherwise one will incur fault. The five things are (1) chewing tooth wood, (2) drinking water, (3) excreting stools, (4) passing water, and (5) performing a *caitya-vandana* (going round a temple) within forty-nine fathoms inside a consecrated boundary.

For instance, when it is time to take a meal, the pupil should go to ask permission of his teacher, whom he should salute according to the rules of salutation, and then say to him, "May my *upādhyāya* be attentive! Now I ask your permission to wash my hands and alms bowl to take a meal." The teacher should say, "Be careful about it!" The permission required for doing other things is asked in the same way. After considering the matter and the time for doing it, the teacher then gives his permission or disallowance.

If the pupil has many things to do, he may ask permission to do all of them at one time.

When, after five summers, the pupil has mastered the Vinaya, he may leave his *upādhyāya* to travel in the world to pursue other subjects of study. But wherever he goes, he must depend on a
222b teacher. It is only after the completion of ten summer [retreats] that he may cease to depend on a teacher. The Great Sage was so thoughtful and considerate as to have laid down this rule. If a monk is not conversant with the Vinaya, he will have to depend on a teacher till the end of his life. If there is no senior teacher available, he may stay with a junior one and do all duties, except salutation, to him. [In that case,] the pupil does not inquire after [his teacher's] health every morning and ask whether he has not lived up to the Vinaya rules. Whenever he has anything to do, he should ask for his teacher's permission. Or he may ask for instructions in the morning and in the evening, but the admonition given at the moment may not be congruent with the intent of the Vinaya. If the pupil who asks for instructions cannot make his point clear, how can the teacher who responds to his request give him any good consultation? This is not the way of asking for instructions. Since such a habit has been handed down for a long time, who would care to take the trouble to make a point-by-point examination of it? If we practice in accordance with the teachings of the Buddha, the Dharma will be maintained without interruption. If one thinks that this is an insignificant matter, what else is important? Thus, it is said in a Vinaya text, "Better to be a butcher than to give full ordination to others and leave them untaught!"

According to the manner of serving one's teacher handed down in India, a pupil should go to his teacher at the first watch and the last watch of the night. The teacher first invites him to sit down comfortably, and then teaches him a passage from the Tripiṭaka (the three collections of the Buddhist canon) that is suitable for the time, leaving no fact or theory unexpounded. He examines his pupil's moral conduct to prevent him from committing defects and violating the disciplinary rules. Whenever he finds that his pupil has committed any fault, he advises him to repent and confess. Then the pupil massages the body of his teacher and folds his robes tidily, or sometimes sweeps the room and the courtyard, and inspects the water to see that no insect is in it before it is sent to the teacher. Whatever is to be done, the pupil does for his teacher. This is how a pupil respects his teacher.

If a pupil falls ill, the teacher personally attends him with medicine and feels such anxiety as he would feel if the pupil were his own child. But according to the guiding principles of the Buddha's teaching, instruction and edification are first and foremost, just as a *cakravartin* (a universal monarch) pays great attention to fostering and educating his eldest son. This is clearly laid down in the Vinaya, and there are no grounds for us to hold it in contempt.

As regards the above-mentioned *caitya-vande* or *caitya-vandana,* it is said that when the Great Teacher, the World-honored One, had entered nirvana, men and gods assembled to cremate his remains. They collected fragrant firewood and built a big funeral pile. That place was known as *citi,* meaning a pile, which gave rise to the name of *caitya*. There are other explanations. First, it is an object which inspires one to meditate that all the virtues of the World-honored One are accumulated here, and second, it is built by piling up bricks and earth. The meaning of the word is handed down as such. Or it is called a stupa, which has the same meaning as *caitya*. Formerly, it was generally called *ta* (pagoda) or *zhi-ti* (a corruption of *caitya*). Both of these terms are incorrect, but both may be used, because people understand what is actually implied without delving into their meanings.

Briefly speaking, there are two ways of explaining a term in India: first, for a term with a meaning, and second, for a term without a meaning. A term that has a meaning has a reason for its coinage, which is interpreted according to its meaning, and the term and its substance are always coincident with each other. For instance, the interpretation of the name Shanru ("well-entering into truth") is that it was first invented according to a man's deeds 222c
of virtue, and so it is a name coined according to its meaning. When

it becomes familiar to the people, they will not delve into its meaning, but call the man "well-entering into truth," simply because the world calls him so. The name becomes thus a term without a meaning.

Vandana means salutation. When one wishes to go out to worship the Buddha's image, if someone inquires, "Where are you going?" one may reply, "I am going to such and such a place to worship the *caitya*." Salutation is a manner of paying respect to one's superiors with a sense of humility. When one is going to pay homage or to ask permission [of one's teacher], one should first adjust one's religious robe to drape over the left shoulder, and press the robe under the left armpit to make it fit tightly to the body, while stretching one's left hand downwards to get hold of the left side of the robe. The right hand follows the robe down to cover the body. When the skirt becomes lower, the robe should be rolled up to the knees, so that both knees are well covered, without exposing the body. The edge of the robe at the back is quickly made to stick to the body. Both the robe and the skirt are held in such a way as not to touch the ground. [When one is kneeling down] the two heels are pointing upwards, with the back and neck in a straight line. The ten fingers are spread on the ground before one bows one's head down, with no part of the robe or anything else used as padding under the knees. One should again join one's hands palm to palm and touch the ground with one's head once more. In this manner one piously makes salutation three times. At ordinary times, one salutation is sufficient; there is no rule that requires one to stand up and then to kneel down again. Should the people of India see one saluting and standing up consecutively three times, they would marvel at it.

If one fears that there might be dust on one's forehead, one may rub it off with one's hand and then wipe it clean. Next, one should wipe away the dust on one's knees. After adjusting one's robe, one should sit at one side or stand for a while. The elder monk should ask him to take a seat, but if the pupil is being reprimanded, it is harmless for him to remain standing. Such is the tradition uninterruptedly handed down from teacher to pupil from the time of the Buddha up to the present age of degeneration. It is said in the scriptures and the Vinaya texts that when one approached the Buddha, one should worship him at his feet and sit down at one side, but it is never mentioned that one should spread the sitting mat, worship three times, and stand at one side. Such is the teaching. In the place where an elder is, many seats should be prepared, so that when people come they may sit in a proper manner. When one sits down, one's feet touch the ground. There is no custom of sitting down with one's knees resting on the ground.

It is said in the Vinaya that one should first assume the *utkuṭaka* posture, which is translated as "a squatting posture," with both feet placed flat on the ground and both knees pointing upwards, the robes being tightly wrapped on the body without falling on the ground. This is the regular posture for performing the ceremony of keeping surplus robes, etc., as pure (legitimate) alms, or making a confession in the presence of other monks, or expressing respect to an assembly, or asking for pardon when one is being reprimanded, or worshiping the monks when receiving full ordination. In all such cases, the posture is the same.

Or one may kneel down on the ground, keeping the back erect with hands joined palm to palm. This is the posture to praise and gaze with reverence at the Buddha's statue on an altar. But worshiping on a couch is not done in any country [except China], nor 223a
does one see the custom of spreading a felt mat [for worshiping]. Is it justifiable to be so insolent while one intends to be respectful? When one is on a couch or a mat, one should not pay respect to others even at ordinary times, let alone when worshiping one's honored teacher or the Great Master. How can such a thing be permissible?

In the lecture halls and dining rooms [of the monasteries] in India, no big couches are provided, but there are a large number of blocks of wood and small chairs prepared for the monks to sit on while listening to a lecture or having a meal. Such was the original custom. In China, the monks have long been used to sitting cross-legged on big couches. Although customs may be changed according to circumstances from time to time, one should know what was the original tradition and what are later derivatives.

26. Conduct towards Visitors and Friends

In the days when the Great Teacher, the founder of the religion, was living in the world, he used to say "welcome" whenever a visiting *bhikṣu* arrived. The monks of the monasteries in India follow the rule that when they see a newcomer arriving, whether he is a visitor, an old friend, a disciple, a pupil, or an acquaintance, they go forward to greet him with the utterance "*Svāgata,*" which is translated as "welcome." Should the newcomer be a guest, the word "*Susvāgata,*" translated as "hearty welcome," must be pronounced. If one does not say these words, one infringes upon the monastic regulations and is also guilty according to the rules of the Vinaya. No matter whether the newcomer is a senior or a junior monk, this is done all the same.

Then [the host] takes off the visitor's water jar and alms bowl, hangs them up on pegs fixed on the wall, and prepares a seat in a proper place for him to rest. If the visitor is a junior monk, he is led to a secluded place, and if he is a senior one, he is invited to sit in the front chamber. If the host is junior to the guest, he should, in honor of his senior, massage his calves up to the whole body. If the host is senior to the guest, he only repeatedly strokes the guest's back, but not down to his waist and feet. If both of them are of the same age, then there will be no difference in the matter.

When [the newcomer] has recovered from fatigue, he washes his hands and feet and proceeds to the superior, whom he worships only once. While kneeling on the ground, he touches the superior's feet. The superior stretches his right hand to stroke the shoulders and back of the guest. But if it has not been a long time since they have seen each other, the superior need not stroke the guest with his hand. Then the teacher inquires after his health, and the disciple answers according to circumstances. After that the guest withdraws to one side and sits down with due respect. There is no custom of standing at one side. The general rule in India is to sit on small blocks of wood, and everybody is barefoot. Since this is not the custom in China, the etiquette of holding another person's feet is not practiced there. It is said in the scriptures that men and gods came to the Buddha, bowed their heads down to his feet, and then withdrew to sit at one side in the manner as mentioned above.

At the chosen time, hot water or other drinks are offered to the guest. Ghee, honey, and granulated sugar may be taken at will. As for the other eight kinds of syrup, they must be filtered and made clear before one drinks them. If they are thick with dregs, they are definitely not allowed [to be taken as beverages].

As the juice of apricots and the like is thick, it is reasonable that it should be totally banned as a beverage. It is said in the Vinaya: "Syrup must be strained until the color becomes as yellowish as the reed." Such are the rites of hospitality for receiving guests in India, whether they are teachers, pupils, visitors, or ac- 223b
quaintances. It is improper for one to perform *he-nan* (salutation) in haste when one has just put down one's garments and cap after arriving at a place, having traveled through severe cold weather or under the scorching sun, with perspiration all over one's body, or with hands and feet benumbed with cold. Such heedless behavior is deeply against the rules of decency. What is more, the teacher allows the guest to stand there gossiping about irrelevant matters. How can such a man of excessive impetuosity be able to make the Dharma continue and prosper?

The word *he-nan* is derived from the Sanskrit *vande* or *vandana* (worshiping), translated as "paying homage." As the transliteration is incorrect, it is pronounced *he-nan*. Since the old transliteration cannot be altered, people still say *he-nan*. If we adopt the correct pronunciation, it should be said as *vande*.

When one is on the road, or in a crowd, it is unsuitable to make salutations; one may just join the hands palm to palm, lower the head, and utter the word *vande*. Thus it is said in a scripture, "Putting the hands together palm to palm, or even lowering the head a little, is also a way of paying homage." People of the south do not know that their behavior seemingly conforms with the regulations. If they could change their unawareness into saying *vande,* their behavior would be perfect, as is ordained in the Vinaya.

27. The Treatment of Disease

As I have said before, one should consider whether one is feeling light or heavy—that is, see whether one's four physical elements are strong or weak—before one takes breakfast. If one feels light and brisk, one may eat the meal as usual, but if anything is wrong, one must find out the cause. When the cause of discomfort has been found, one should rest. When one is feeling light and healthy, one will feel as hungry as if a fire were burning inside, and then one may take food at breakfast time. Daybreak is usually called "the time of phlegm," when the remnant fluid of food taken before the night is still crammed in the chest and has not yet dispersed; food taken at this time is a cause of trouble. It is just like throwing fuel into a blazing fire. The fuel will be consumed by the flames, but if straw is placed on a fire not yet brightly burning, the straw will remain there, while the fire will not burn.

Breakfast is specially permitted by the Buddha. Whether it is porridge or cooked rice, the meal is taken according to one's physical condition. If one can subsist on porridge alone in order to practice the Way, one may just eat it without taking anything else. If one wishes to eat cooked rice for the nourishment of the body, it is harmless to take cooked rice in the morning. If any food causes discomfort to the body, it is a source of illness. Do not say that one is ill when one only has a headache or is lying in bed. When no other medicine is curative, a physician may prescribe "untimely food" for the patient, and the Buddha said that it might be served in a secluded place. No monk is allowed to take food at irregular hours except by the prescription of a physician.

According to the lore of medicine, one of the five lores of India, a physician should first examine the voice and countenance of his

patient, and then prescribe for him in accordance with the eight branches of medical knowledge. If he does not understand the secret of this knowledge, he will cause adverse effects though he intended to produce advantageous results. The eight branches of medical knowledge are: (1) the treatment of all kinds of ulcers; (2) the treatment of ailments of the head by acupuncture; (3) the treatment of diseases of the body; (4) the treatment of illnesses caused
by demons; (5) the treatment of sickness with *agada* (antidotal) 223c
medicine; (6) the treatment of children's diseases; (7) the art of longevity; and (8) the method of strengthening the legs and body.

Ulcers are of two kinds, internal and external. Ailments of the head are those illnesses that trouble only the head. Diseases below the neck are called bodily diseases. Discomfort caused by demons is a complaint induced by evil demons. *Agada* is a panacea for counteracting all kinds of poison. The word "children" indicates infants from the stage of an embryo up to the age of sixteen years. Longevity means to keep the body healthy so as to live long. When the legs are energetic, the body will be strong and healthy. These eight arts of healing were formerly contained in eight books. Lately they have been abridged into one bundle [of palm leaves].

In the five parts of India, [all physicians] practice medicine according to this book. The physicians who are well learned in it are all paid with official salaries. Therefore, physicians are greatly honored in India. Merchants and traders are also held in esteem, as they do not injure life but benefit themselves and help others at the same time. I have also spent some time in studying the lore of medicine, but as it was not my proper duty I abandoned the pursuit at last.

Moreover, we should know that the medicinal herbs of India are different from those of China. What is found in one country may not be found in the other, and so they are not the same in the two countries. For instance, such herbs as ginseng, tuckahoe, Chinese angelica, polygala, aconite, monkshood, Chinese ephedra, asarum, and the like are the best medicinal herbs in China, but I did not see any of them when I made inquiries about them in India. In India there is abundant *harītakī* (yellow myrobalan), and in the northern part one may sometimes find turmeric, while the western frontier is rich in ferula. A small quantity of camphor is produced in [the islands of] the South Seas. All three species of cardamom are grown in Dvārapati, while the two kinds of cloves are produced in the country of Kun-lun. Only these herbs are needed in China; all other medicinal herbs are not worth gathering.

When the body, which is made up of the four elements, is ill, the illness is caused in all cases by overeating or fatigue, or by taking a meal early in the morning when the food taken before the night has not been discharged, or by eating again at noon when breakfast has not been digested. For these reasons, cholera develops. One belches consecutively for several nights, and the belly is swollen for more than ten days. Then one seeks expensive medicines to cure the kidneys and tries to get costly *Gentiana macrophylla*. A rich man can afford to do so, but a poor man can live only as long as the morning dew. What can one do to save the life of such a poor man when he is attacked by illness? Even if a good physician came in the morning to offer pills and medicinal powder, they would be of no effect. Even if Bianque [the highly skilled physician] visited him in the evening with medical decoctions and plasters, he could not save his life. Moxibustion and acupuncture applied to him are just as if put on wood or stone. He could only shake his legs and head; otherwise he would be no different from a corpse.

All this is due to ignorance of the causes of illness and not understanding how to take good care of oneself so as to recuperate. It is like trying to stop a stream without damming up its source, or cutting a tree without removing its roots, so that the current will spread and the branches will sprout again without being extirpated. The result is that those who engage in studying the scriptures and commentaries only gaze at the Tripiṭaka with ceaseless sighs [over their enfeebled bodies], and those who practice meditation can only imagine the mental state of the eight kinds of *samādhi* (intent concentration) with long lamentations. Lay scholars who aim at

achieving the Doctorate of Classics curb their bridles at the Gate 224a
of the Golden Horse [being prevented by illness from entering that government house], and those who are trying to compete for the position of Advanced Scholar halt outside the Shi-qu-ge (the Imperial Library). Is it not a great hindrance that impedes one from cultivating the Way and performing good deeds? It is not, indeed, a small matter to lose one's good repute and glory. So I have made this narration—I hope that my readers will not deem it prolix and repetitious—so that chronic complaints may be cured without the treatment of a physician. When the four elements [of the physical body] are well regulated, one will never be affected by any kind of disease. Is it not beneficial to do good for oneself as well as others?

If one is poisoned to death [in the course of taking medicine], it is the result of one's deeds done in a previous life. Yet, in our present life, it is necessary to avoid [what is undesirable] and take [what is beneficial].

28. Rules for Taking Medicine

All living creatures without exception are liable to suffer from ailments caused by disorders of the four elements; and the eight seasonal changes, coming one after another, may induce illness at no fixed time. Whenever one is ill, one should rest at once. Therefore, the World-honored One said when delivering the *Sutra on Medical Prescriptions:* "The disorders of the four elements are as follows: (1) *guru* (indigestion), (2) *kapha* (phlegm), (3) *pitta* (bile), and (4) *vata* (wind)." The first is an increase of the element of earth, which causes the body to feel heavy; the second is an accumulation of the element of water, which causes excessive snivel and saliva; the third is the burning of the element of fire, which makes the head and chest strongly feverish; and the fourth is a great agitation of the element of wind, which makes one pant with a striking and rushing breath. These four correspond with what are known in China as serious heaviness, phlegmatic illness, yellow fever, and the bursting of breath. But if we discuss disease according to popular pathology, there are only three kinds of illness, namely, ailments caused by wind, feverish maladies, and phlegmatic sickness. Serious heaviness is substantially identical with phlegmatic illness, without being separately elucidated as pertaining to the element of earth.

In order to find out the cause of a disease, one should examine oneself early in the morning. If one feels that the four elements are abnormal or out of order, one should first refrain from eating. Even if one is very thirsty, one must not drink any juice or water. This utmost abstinence should be observed for one or two days, or sometimes for four or five days, until the disease is cured. This is the right thing for one to do, but there is no fixed duration for it. If one feels that there is food remaining undigested in the stomach, one should press the navel and the chest with one's fingers stretched like a fork. It is good for one to drink a large quantity of hot water and thrust a finger into the throat to cause the food to eject out. One should drink water again and vomit once more, till the stomach is completely emptied. Drinking cold water is also harmless. Hot water with dry ginger soaked in it is a wonderful cure. On that day food must be cut off, and one may break the fast on the following morning. If it is difficult for one to fast for a day, temporary adjustments may be arranged according to circumstances. If one is having a high fever, one should particularly avoid taking a cold shower bath. If one feels seriously heavy and is shivering with cold, it is good for one to remain near a fire, but this is inapplicable in the hot and damp places south of the Yangzi River and in the Five Ranges. It is the local custom of these places to take a cold shower bath when one is having a fever.

In the case of acute rheumatoid arthritis, ointment may be applied, and it is also good to use a hot ball of cloth to heat the affected part of the body. The application of heated oil will produce an immediate effect.

One may feel phlegm filling the chest, with saliva oozing incessantly out of the mouth, and clear mucus flowing from the nose.

Breath may accumulate in the pharynx. The throat is sometimes choked when the mouth is overfull with food so that one cannot 224b speak properly, and food and drink become tasteless for as long as some ten days. Merely by fasting, such complaints may be cured without taking the trouble of cauterizing the head, nor is it necessary to resort to massaging the throat. Such are the general principles by which medicine can cure a disease without using medical decoctions.

I conjecture that when undigested food is removed, high fever will abate, and that when the flowing saliva is exhausted, phlegmatic disease will be cured. If the internal organs remain quiet, and evil air is dispersed, violent wind will cease by itself. Nothing will go wrong if one regulates the physique in this manner. One need not trouble a physician to feel one's pulse, nor is it needful to consult a witch doctor. Each person is then a king of physicians, and everyone becomes a Jīvaka [a well-known physician at the time of the Buddha].

As regards the method of the Dharma master Tanluan, who could cure his own ailments by regulating his breath, it could be practiced only by hermits. The Dhyāna master Huisi could extract evil influences from his body by composing his mind in abstract meditation, but this is unknowable to common people. If it is necessary to consult a reputable physician in the eastern capital of Luo-yang, a poor man will be stopped at the ford [for want of money to pay the boatman]. When it is necessary to seek the best herbs in the western suburbs, the solitary and childless will lose their way. The fasting mentioned above costs no money and is wonderful as a treatment. As it can be applied by both the rich and the poor, is it not an important remedy?

With the abrupt appearance of carbuncle or acne, hot blood will rush up all of a sudden, and both the hands and feet will feel irritated and painful. At the moment when such diseases as the plague, punishments sent by heaven, bodily wounds caused by a sword or an arrow, fractures resulting from stumbling and falling, typhoid fever, acute gastroenteritis, half-day diarrhea, headaches, angina pectoris, sores around the eyes, toothaches, and the like, have begun to arise, one should start fasting.

A pill made of three components will cure various diseases, and it is not difficult to obtain. Take *harītakī* bark, dry ginger, and granulated sugar, all equal in quantity. Pound the first two into powder, and then mix the powder with the sugar in a few drops of water to knead the mixture into pills. About ten pills in the morning is the limit, and one is not to abstain from eating. No more than two or three doses will be sufficient to cure a patient with diarrhea. It will break up gas in the stomach, disperse cold, and help digestion. As it is widely useful, I have mentioned it here. If no granulated sugar is available, maltose or honey will do. If one could chew one piece of *harītakī* and swallow the juice every day, one would be free from disease throughout one's whole life.

This medical lore was handed down by Indra. As one of the five sciences, it is practiced in all of the five parts of India. Among its methods of treatment, the most important one is fasting. The old translators said that when a patient was not cured after having fasted for seven days, he might invoke the aid of Avalokiteśvara. In China, most people do not understand this method and think of it as a separate system of religious fasting; thus they do not care to study it. This is because the translators did not understand the art of healing. Those who suffer from illnesses caused by taking cinnabar and crystal [for immortality], or from a chronic disease, such as a lump in the belly, may also apply this method. (Yijing's running note: But I fear that it might be unsuitable for those who take cinnabar and crystal to go hungry. The cinnabar drug that enables one to levitate is not found in any other country, and the eating of [pulverized] crystal is practiced only in China. But some kinds of crystal or moonstone may produce fire, and if they are taken, the body will explode. As people of the present day cannot distinguish them, numerous men have died in vain [of this bad practice]. Thus we should be deeply aware of the harmfulness of this.)

Poisoning caused by snakebite or scorpion sting cannot be cured by this treatment [fasting]. When one is fasting, roaming about and doing hard work should be strictly avoided. A long-distance traveler may go on his way without harm even if he is fasting, but he should rest after his recuperation, and eat newly cooked rice or drink any amount of well-boiled mung bean soup, seasoned with fragrant giant hyssop. If he feels chilly, he may add pepper, ginger, and *Piper longum* to the soup. If he knows that it is a cold, scallion and *Nepeta japonica* should be put into the soup. It is said in a work on medicine that all pungent things are liable to promote cold, with the exception of dry ginger, and so it is also good to add them to the soup. On days of fasting, one should regulate one's breath and abstain from drinking cold water. Other abstentions are just the same as taking regular medicine, but if one is sure to be suffering from cold, one may take porridge without harm. In the case of suffering from fever, it is good to drink well-boiled decoctions of the root of bitter ginseng (*Sophora flavescens*). Tea is also good. For more than twenty years after I left my native country, I only drank this as a medicinal beverage to preserve my health, and I scarcely suffered from any disease. 224c

The medicines in China, including the stone needle for acupuncture, amount to more than four hundred kinds of herbs consisting of roots and stalks of different plants, most of which are fine and rare in color and have a fragrant flavor. They are effective for curing diseases and can invigorate one's spirit. Acupuncture and the skill of feeling the pulse [in China] are never surpassed by any country in Jambudvīpa, and the drugs for long life are found only in China. Because our hills are connected with the Himalayas and our mountains are linked with the Gandhamādanas, many strange and precious things are produced here in abundance. On account of the natural disposition of her people and the quality of her products, China is known as the Divine Land. In all the five parts of India, who does not esteem China, and who within the four seas does not hold her in respect? It is said that Mañjuśrī is now living in that country. Wherever a monk goes, if the people hear that he is a monk from the Devaputra, they will worship him with great honor. *Deva* means "heaven," and *putra* "a son," denoting that he is coming from the place of the Son of Heaven in China.

The medicinal herbs and the acupuncture [used in China] are really wonderful, but recuperative measures and the discovery of the causes of disease are very much neglected. So I am here giving a rough description of how to meet the need in time. If fasting fails to alleviate one's ailment, one may then resort to medical treatment according to a prescription. A decoction of bitter ginseng is a specific remedy for feverish diseases, while ghee, honey, and fruit juice are particularly good for curing colds. In the country of Lāṭa in West India, people who are ill abstain from food for a fortnight, or a full month, and will take food only after they have been cured of their illness. In Central India the limit for fasting is seven days, and in the South Seas it is but two or three days. This is because of different local conditions and variant physical constitutions. So the number of days for fasting is more in one place and less at another, without a uniform limit.

I do not know whether or not fasting is suitable to be practiced in China. Most people die after abstaining from food for seven days, but this is because one is not afflicted with any illness. But if one is infected with illness, one will not die even [after fasting] for many days. Once I saw a sick man who fasted for thirty days and recovered afterwards. So it is not surprising to see one fasting for many
225a days. How can one force a man to drink hot porridge in spite of his sickness, simply on seeing that he is attacked by a burning fever, without examining the cause of his illness? Such an act is deeply dreadful! If by any chance one is cured by such a treatment, it is after all not to be taught to the laypeople. It is strictly prohibited to do so in the lore of medicine.

Furthermore, the people of present-day China mostly eat raw fish and vegetables, but the Indians never eat anything uncooked. All sorts of vegetables are well cooked and mixed with ferula, ghee, and spices before being eaten, and they never eat pickles or mincemeat made of pickles. I remember once I ate some of these things, and they caused me to suffer from a painful lump in the abdomen, which hurt my belly, clogged my intestines, induced sore eyes, and enfeebled me all the more. That is why the Indians do not eat them. Wise people should consider the matter well as to what is useful and practicable, and what should be abandoned or be kept in mind. If one has heard the advice of a physician, but does not act accordingly, is the physician to be blamed? If one acts in accordance with medical advice, one will live at ease and be able to follow the Way in a perfect manner, benefiting both oneself and others. If one abandons good advice, one will have a weak body and be feeble-minded, while all one's efforts to do good for oneself and others will be lost.

29. Avoidance of Evil Drugs

At certain places where the vulgar custom has long been prevalent, the people take feces and urine in time of illness, and when a disease comes on, the dung of pigs or cats is used. Such things, entitled "dragon decoctions," are kept in an urn or a jar. In spite of their nice name, they are the worst of all filthy things. Even after eating onion or garlic, which are permissible for a monk to eat, one has to stay in a side room to purify oneself by washing and bathing for seven days before joining others. When one's body is not yet purified, one should not enter the assembly of monks, nor is it fitting for one to walk round a stupa. One must not worship [an image of the Buddha]. Owing to their offensive smell, a monk is not allowed to eat these things, unless he is ill.

What is called "putrid-discharged[-medicine]," which is one of the four dependences, is the medicine which is putrid and discharged [by a cow]. It is meant to save trouble and get what is merely for the preservation of the body. Costly medicine is, of course, allowable, and there is no harm in taking it. In the Sanskrit term *pūti-mukti-bhaiṣajya, pūti* means "putrid," *mukti* is "discharged," and *bhaiṣajya* is translated as "medicine." (Yijing's running note: Thus we have "putrid-discharged-medicine.")

The Vinaya permits feces and urine to be used as medicine, but the dung of a calf and the urine of a cow are meant. In India, the body of one who is condemned to capital punishment is smeared with [human] feces and discarded in the wilderness outside human habitation. Night-soil removers and scavengers strike sticks to distinguish themselves while going about. If anybody touches them accidentally, he has to wash himself and his garments thoroughly clean.

It was the principle of the Great Teacher to act according to circumstances and take precautions against people's derision and slander. How could he have asked others to take such things against the customs of his time? The reasons for his disallowance are fully explained in the Vinaya. It is really despicable for one to give such things to others for their use. We should not allow vulgar customs to become a regular practice. If foreigners heard about it, it would be detrimental to the good name of our morals and manners. Moreover, we have plenty of fragrant medicinal herbs, and why should we not use them? Why should one give others what one does not
225b take for oneself? To counteract the poison of snakebite, we have such minerals as sulfur, realgar, and orpiment, and it is not difficult to get pieces of them and take them with us. If one is suffering from miasma fever, there are such febrifuges as the decoction prepared with licorice, [the wild tea of] Mount Heng, and bitter ginseng, which may be kept in large or small quantities and are easily obtainable. Colds can be completely cured by taking some ginger, pepper, or *Piper longum* in the morning. Rock candy and granulated sugar, when eaten at night, may satiate hunger and thirst. If nothing is laid aside to meet the cost of medicine, one will certainly be short of money in time of need. If one acts contrary to the teaching [of the Buddha] and does not put the teaching into practice, how can one be free from committing faults? When money is squandered aimlessly, one will be in a tight corner in an emergency. Who can have a direct understanding of this, if I do not explain it in detail? Alas! People do not utilize good medicine but, in order to save trouble, they use the "dragon decoction"! Although

they have some small benefit in mind, they are not aware that it is a great offense against the holy teaching. Followers of the Sāṃmitīya School speak of the putrid-discharged-medicine, but as it is a different school from ours, we should not follow its example. Although it is mentioned in the *Vinaya-dvāviṃśati-prasannārtha-śāstra,* this is not a work studied by the adherents of the Sarvāstivāda School.

30. On Turning to the Right and the Observation of Time

Turning to the right is *pradakṣiṇa* in Sanskrit. The prefix *pra* has various meanings, but here in this word it denotes "going round." *Dakṣiṇa* means "the right side," generally signifying what is respectable and dexterous. Thus my contemporaries [in India] call the right hand the *dakṣiṇa* hand, meaning that it is on the right side and is respectable and dexterous. It is, therefore, in conformity with the rites of walking round [a respectable person or object]. *Dakṣiṇa* also means a donation to the monks, and in this case it is different in meaning from what is mentioned here, as I have explained before. In all the five parts of India, the east is called the front, and the south is at one's right side, but this is not the point by which to decide what is right and left [when going round a respectable person or object].

In the scriptures it should be said that one walked round [the Buddha] three times towards the right side, but it is wrong to say that one walked beside the Buddha. In some scriptures it is said that one walked round three times towards the right side, and this is in conformity with the rites. It is an abridgment to say that one walked round a hundred or a thousand times without saying "towards the right."

It is somewhat difficult to decide which is walking round towards the right and which is towards the left. Shall we deem walking towards one's right hand to be towards the right, and walking towards one's left hand to be towards the left? Once a Chinese scholar elucidated the point, saying that when one's right hand is towards the interior of the circle in going round an object, it is called right side circumambulation, and when the left hand is towards the interior of the circle, it is called left side circumambulation. He argued that one can complete right side circumambulation only by walking round an object towards its left side. This is merely his conjecture. It is irrelevant to the correct theory, and it misguided ignorant people. Even some men of great virtue and erudition are so puzzled as to echo that scholar's opinion.

What shall we do to make a compromise according to reason? We should depend upon only the Sanskrit texts and stop up our personal feelings. To walk round towards the right side [of a person or an object of veneration] is right side circumambulation, while to walk towards the left side is left side circumambulation. This is the rule laid down by the Holy One, and there is no doubt about it.

225c As regards what are [proper] and what are improper times, there are various implications according to different circumstances, as is explained in the *Scripture on Proper Times and Improper Times*. But in the Vinaya texts of the four schools, it is unanimously affirmed that noontime is the proper time [for taking a meal]. If the shadow of the needle on a sundial has passed even as little as a thread, it is considered an improper time. If a person wishes to determine the cardinal points in order to guard himself against committing the fault [of eating at an improper time], he should measure the north star and observe the southern constellation at night, so as to fix the correct line [between the south and the north poles], and to find out when noontime is approaching. Again, he may also build a small earthen mound, one foot in diameter and five inches in height, at a key position. At the center of the mound a slender stick is inserted. Or a nail is sometimes fixed on a piece of stone. It is as slim as a bamboo chopstick, four finger-widths in length. A line is to be drawn over the shadow of the nail at the moment of high noon. If the shadow has passed the line, it becomes improper for one to eat food. In India such a sundial, known as a *velācakra,* translated as a round instrument for marking time, is set up in most places. The purpose of measuring the shadow is to find out when it is at its shortest, which marks the moment of the meridian.

But in Jambudvīpa the midday line varies in measurement at different locations. For instance, in the region of Luo there is no shadow at all, and this is different from other regions. Again, in the country of Śrībhoja, the shadow on the sundial is neither long nor short in the middle of the eighth moon. At midday a man, or any object under the sun, casts no shadow on the ground. Such is also the case in the middle of spring. The sun passes overhead twice a year. When the sun is traveling in the south, the shadow [of a man] falls northwards and is two or three feet in length. When it is in the north, the shadow is the same towards the south. In China, the shadow towards the south and that towards the north are different [in length], and doors with the north at the back always face the sun. When it is midday on the eastern coast of China, it is not yet noontime in the western part of the country. Since it is difficult to hold one principle for all matters, it is said in the Vinaya: "When time is to be determined, one should do so according to the [local] zenith, and then the time is fixed."

All homeless monks should behave according to the holy teaching. As taking food is absolutely necessary every day, one should be mindful about measuring the shadow before eating. If one neglected this rule, how could one observe the other precepts? Therefore, those eminent monks who are engaged in propagating the Dharma and making it prosperous never complain of the minute and complicated [disciplinary rules]. Even when they are traveling on the sea, they carry the sundial with them; will they go without it when they are on land? In India, tradition says that one who inspects the water [to ensure that it is free from insects] and affirms that it is high noon is a master of Vinaya.

Furthermore, clepsydras are kept in all the large monasteries in India. They are gifts donated by successive generations of kings, together with watchers, to keep the monks informed of the hours.

The lower part of the device is a copper vessel filled with water on which a copper bowl is floating. The bowl is thin and delicately made, capable of holding two *sheng*s (one *sheng* equals one liter) of water, with a hole as tiny as a pinhole at the bottom, from which water leaks in. It is an accurate device for the measurement of time. When the bowl is full of water, it sinks, and a drum is sounded. Commencing at dawn, one stroke of the drum is sounded at the first sinking of the bowl, two strokes at the second sinking, and
226a three strokes at the third sinking. After the four strokes of the drum at the fourth sinking, a conch is blown twice, ending with one more stroke of the drum, indicating the first hour, when the sun is rising in the east. After the second round of the bowl sinking four times and the drum being beaten four times with the conch being blown once more, the drum is sounded twice to indicate the second hour; this marks the exact moment of high noon. When the drum has been struck twice, the monks should stop eating. If anyone is found eating, he is expelled [from the community of monks] according to monastic regulations. In the afternoon, there are also two hours, announced in the same way as in the forenoon. The four hours of the night are similar to those in the daytime. As a whole, one day and one night consist of eight hours.

At the end of the first watch, the director of duties strikes a drum in a loft of the monastery to announce the time for the monks. Such is the way of using the clepsydra in Nālandā Monastery. At dusk and dawn, a drum is beaten for one stretch at the gate. These miscellaneous affairs are performed by servants or porters. From sunset to dawn, the ordinary monks are not obliged to sound the *ghaṇṭā* (bell), nor is it the duty of servants; the director of duties has to do it himself. There is a difference between beating four or five strokes [on the *ghaṇṭā*], and it is fully explained elsewhere.

The clepsydras are somewhat different in the monasteries in Mahābodhi and Kuśinagara, where the bowls sink sixteen times between dawn and midday. In the country of Ku-lun in the South Seas, a copper cauldron filled with water is used, and the water leaks down through a tiny hole at the bottom. When the water is drained away, the drum will be sounded. Each time the cauldron is emptied, the drum is beaten once, and when the drum has been beaten four times, it is midday. This process is repeated till sunset. At night there are also eight hours as in the daytime, and there are sixteen hours altogether [in a day and a night]. These clepsydras are also gifts presented by the king of that country.

It is due to the use of the clepsydra that one is never perplexed about noontime even on a dark day with thick clouds overhead, and that during a night of continuous rain there is no doubt about the watches. We should also present a memorial to the [Chinese] emperor, asking for the installation [of clepsydras in our monasteries], as it is an important piece of equipment for monks.

In making a clepsydra one should first divide a day and a night in such a way as to let the bowl sink eight times from dawn to noontime. If it is to sink fewer than eight times, the hole in the bowl should be drilled bigger. A skillful mechanic is required to regulate the device correctly. When the day or night gradually becomes shorter, half a spoonful of water is added to the device. When they become gradually longer, half a flagon of water is taken out. But this is done within the limit of increments or decrements of time. It is reasonable for the director of duties to keep a small bowl [to mark the time] in his chamber without incurring any fault.

In China there are five watches [in the night], and in India there are four parts, but according to the teaching of the Buddha, the Tamer of Men, there are three hours in the night, i.e., a night is divided into three parts. During the first and third parts, one should recite [the holy texts], and only during the second part may one sleep with a concentrated mind. One who deviates from this rule incurs the fault of violating the Buddha's teaching, unless he is ill. If one puts this into practice with a mind of veneration, one will ultimately benefit oneself and others.

End of Fascicle Three

Fascicle Four

31. Bathing the Buddha's Image

It has been explained in detail that none is more venerable than 226b
the three honored ones, and that nothing can surpass the four noble truths as subjects for meditation. But the intrinsic principle of the truths is so profound that it is beyond the understanding of an uncultivated mind, while the lavation of the holy image [of the Buddha] can be performed with benefit by all people. Although the Great Teacher has entered nirvana, his image still exists, and we should venerate it as if he were in the world. Incense and flowers should often be offered to the image; by doing so our mind may be purified. To bathe it regularly is good enough to clear away the evil influence of our deeds caused by idleness. With this point in mind, one will receive invisible benefits, and if one advises others to do so, one will gain visible advantages both for oneself and for others. I hope that those who wish to obtain bliss will bear this practice in mind.

In the monasteries of India, at the time for bathing the Buddha's image, usually in the forenoon, the director of duties strikes a *ghaṇṭā*. (Yijing's running note: The director of duties, or the giver of duties, is *karmadāna* in Sanskrit. *Dāna* means "giving," and *karma,* "action," i.e., one who gives various duties to the monks. This term was formerly rendered as *wei-na,* which is incorrect. In Chinese, the character *wei* means "a cord" or "to tie together," while *na* stands for the last syllable of the Sanskrit *karmadāna,* and was used as an abbreviation of the word.) A precious canopy is stretched in the court of the monastery, and bottles containing perfumed water are put in a row by the side of the shrine hall. An image of the Buddha, made of either gold, silver, bronze, or stone, is placed in a basin of copper, gold, wood, or stone, while dancing girls are asked to play music. The image is rubbed with scented paste, and then perfumed water is poured over it. (Yijing's running note: Take any scented wood, such as sandalwood or aloeswood, and grind it with water into paste on a flat stone which [looks like] a plinth. The image is rubbed with this paste before perfumed water is poured over it.) It is then wiped clean with a piece of pure white cloth and set up in the shrine hall, which is decorated with flowers and colored ribbons. This is the ceremony performed by the monks of a monastery under the guidance of the director of duties. In their separate rooms the monks also perform this ceremony in an individual way, and they do so every day without negligence, regarding it as important.

All kinds of flowers, either from herbs or trees, may be used as offerings. Whether in the winter or in the summer, there are always fragrant flowers, and there are also many flower sellers in the markets. In China, for instance, lotuses and pinks display various colors in summer and autumn, while golden vitex, peach, and apricot trees bloom profusely in the springtime. The althaea bushes
226c and pomegranate trees blossom one after the other at different times, and the red cherry and white crab apple trees put forth new buds from season to season. Such flowers as those from hollyhocks in gardens or from vanilla trees in the villages must be brought in and properly arranged [before the image]; they should not be left in gardens for one to view from afar. In the winter when flowers may run short for some time, we may cut colored silk [into artificial flowers] and mix them with powdered perfume. It is really good to place them before the image of the Buddha.

The bronze images, regardless of size, must be polished brightly with fine brick dust, and then pure water is poured over them, until they become as clear and brilliant as a mirror. A large image must be washed as a joint effort by all of the monks in the middle and at the end of each month, while a small one may be washed every day by an individual monk according to his ability. Although the cost of this performance is small, the bliss and benefit gained therefrom are great.

The water in which an image has been bathed is known as the water of auspiciousness. One may wish for success by sprinkling it with two fingers over one's head. One should not smell the flowers that have been offered to an image, nor should one trample on them when they are taken off [the altar], but they should be put away in a clean place. How can a monk be allowed not to bathe the holy image during his lifetime till his hair has turned white? Although red flowers may be spread all over the fields, he has no mind to pick them as offerings to an image. Thus he becomes lazy in performing [religious functions], and when people point out [lotus] ponds and gardens, he remains indolent and shirks the bore [of picking flowers]. He is so idle as to be reluctant to open the Buddha hall, and is contented with collective worship. In this manner the line of succession from teacher to pupil will be broken, and there will be nowhere to pay homage [to the Buddha].

It is the duty of monks and laymen in India to build *caitya*s with clay and mold images out of clay, or to print [images] on silk or paper to be worshiped wherever one goes, or to pile up heaps of clay and surround them with bricks to form stupas in the wilderness, to be left there to fall apart and disappear naturally. (There is a Chinese note.)

When they make an image or build a *caitya* out of gold, silver, copper, iron, clay, lacquer, bricks, or stone, or even by piling up sand or snow, they put two kinds of relics inside them. One is the Great Teacher's relic bones, and the other is the verse on dependent origination, which reads:

> All things arise from conditions;
> The Tathāgata has expounded the causes.
> All things end with the end of the conditions.
> Thus was spoken by the Great *Śramaṇa*.

If these two kinds of relics are placed inside the image or *caitya,* one will gain plenty of bliss. Therefore, many parables are widely used in the scriptures to praise the unthinkable advantages of doing so. If a man makes an image even as small as a grain of barley, or builds a *caitya* as tiny as a jujube with a wheel sign and a spire as little as a pin on it, he will obtain special good causes as limitless as the seven seas, and his good rewards will last as long as four rebirths. A full account of this matter is given in detail in separate scriptures.

I hope various teachers will perform this function from time to time. To bathe and venerate a holy image is an action that makes one meet a Buddha in all lives, and the offering of flowers and incense is a cause for one to enjoy wealth and happiness in all future rebirths. Whether one does the work oneself or advises others to do it, one will get unlimited bliss.

I have seen in some places that the monks or laymen brought
227a out an image to the roadside, poured water over it and washed it properly, but they did not know how to dry it with a wiper. They simply exposed the image to the sun to be dried by the wind. This is incongruous with the rites.

32. The Ceremony of Chanting

It is a tradition handed down from ancient times in the Divine Land that the monks worship the Buddha by repeating his name; most of them do not extol him and praise his virtues. One may only listen to the repetition of his name and not know the height of his wisdom, but when his virtues are praised and fully enumerated, one will realize the greatness and depth of his virtues. In India the monks practice *caitya-vandana* (walking round a *caitya*) and pay regular homage late in the afternoon or in the evening. The monks gather in an assembly, go out of the gate [of the monastery], and walk three times round a stupa to which incense and flowers are offered. Then they crouch on the ground, and a competent monk is asked to praise the virtues of the Buddha in ten or twenty stanzas, with a lamenting and elegant voice and in a clear and solemn manner.

After that they return in regular sequence to the usual meeting place in the monastery. Having taken their seats, they invite a scripture-reciter to mount the lion seat to read a short scripture. The lion seat, which is well proportioned, being neither too high nor too big, is placed at the head of the line of seats, with the chief monk's seat next to it. The recitation mostly consists of three statements selected and arranged by the Venerable Aśvaghoṣa. The first statement, containing about ten stanzas, is a hymn praising the three honored ones according to the contents of the scriptures. The second statement is the full text of the scripture recited, which consists of the words of the Buddha. After the conclusion of the hymn and the reading of the scripture, a resolution is made in more than ten stanzas for the transference of merits. As the recitation is divided into three sections, it is known as the three statements.

When the recitation is over, all the monks in the assembly exclaim *"Subhāṣita!" Su* means "well," and *bhāṣita,* "spoken," that is, "Well-spoken!" Their intention is to praise the scripture as a text of wonderful sayings. Or they exclaim *"Sādhu,"* meaning "Excellent!"

When the scripture-reciter has descended, the chief monk rises first to salute the lion seat, and then salutes the seats of the holy monks. After doing so, he resumes his own seat. The monk second in order salutes the two places as the chief monk did and also worships the chief monk; then he returns to his own seat. The monk who is third in order performs the rites in the same manner. This is done by all the other monks till the last one has made his homage. If the assembly is too large, after three or five persons have performed the ceremony mentioned above, all the rest may salute the assembly collectively at one and the same time, and then they retire at will. This is the normal practice for performing the ceremony of the monks of Tāmralipti in eastern India.

In Nālandā Monastery where there are so many resident monks that they exceed three thousand in number, it is difficult to assemble all the monks in a hurry. There are eight courtyards with

three hundred rooms, but the monks may perform the rites of paying homage and recitation at any time in their separate places. It is the custom of this monastery to appoint a preacher capable of chanting to go round from place to place every evening to conduct the ceremony of worshiping and praising [the virtues of the Buddha], with a servant and a boy holding incense and flowers leading the way. He goes through every courtyard and pays homage in all the shrine halls. Each time he pays homage, he chants the praises of the
227b Buddha in three or five stanzas in a high voice that is heard all around. He completes the round in the twilight. This preacher always receives special offerings provided by the monastery.

One may sit alone, facing the shrine, and praise the Buddha in his mind, or go to a temple and kneel on the ground together with others to chant in a high pitch. One may then put one's hands on the ground and touch it with one's head three times. This is the traditional ceremony of paying homage practiced in India. The aged and sick monks may be allowed to use small seats [while performing the ceremony]. We [in China] have had the stanzas in praise of the Buddha since ancient times, but our way of chanting them is somewhat different from that of the Brahmanic land of India. For instance, when the stanza in praise of the Buddha's excellent physical marks is chanted while worshiping the Buddha, it is intoned in an even tone with a long trailing voice, in ten or twenty verses. This is the proper way of chanting it. Moreover, the hymn in praise of the Tathāgata, etc., is really sung to extol the Buddha, but as the intonation is somewhat prolonged, the meaning becomes difficult for one to understand. When the assembly of monks is feeling sad on a quiet night on the day of performing ceremonies in memory of the dead, it is really good to ask a competent monk to recite the *Hymn of One Hundred and Fifty Verses* and the *Hymn of Four Hundred Verses*, as well as other panegyrics.

In India, numerous panegyrics have been handed down to be sung when paying homage, and there was no man of literary talent who did not compose an encomium in praise of a person whom he deemed worthy to be eulogized. The Venerable Mātṛceṭa was such a man of great talent and high virtue, who excelled above all scholars of good learning of his time. Tradition says that when the Buddha was living, he once led a group of disciples, wandering among the people. An oriole, on seeing the features of the Buddha as magnificent as a golden mountain, began to trill melodiously in the wood as if it were eulogizing him. The Buddha looked back and said to his disciples, "This bird is so delighted with my appearance that it can't help warbling in a quavering manner. Owing to this good deed, it shall be reborn, after my departure from the world, in the form of a man with the name of Mātṛceṭa, who will extensively exalt me for my great virtues." (Yijing's running note: *Mātṛi* means "mother," and *ceṭa,* "child.")

At first this man became an ascetic of a heretical religion and worshiped Maheśvara. Since this deity was the object of his veneration, he composed hymns in praise of him. Afterwards, when he saw that his name had been mentioned in a prediction, he turned his mind to believe in the Buddha and dyed his garment to live as a monk away from secular life. He widely glorified the Buddha, repenting what wrongs he had done in the past and desiring to follow the superior Way in the future. He regretted that he had not met the Great Teacher in person but had only seen his image. Thus he wrote, in accordance with the prediction, encomiums in an ornate style to extol the virtues of the Buddha. He composed first the *Hymn of Four Hundred Verses* and then the *Hymn of One Hundred and Fifty Verses,* both for the elucidation of the six *pāramitā*s (the six perfect virtues) and for the exposition of the superior virtues of the Buddha, the World-honored One. These compositions are graceful and brilliant in phraseology, equal in beauty to heavenly blossoms, and the principles contained in them are so lofty as to rival earthly mountains in height. All eulogists in India imitated his style and regarded him as the father of eulogistic literature, and both Asaṅga and Vasubandhu greatly ad- 227c
mired him. In all the five parts of India those who become monks are first taught these two compositions as soon as they can recite

the five and ten precepts, this being the rule for all monks regardless of whether they belong to the Mahayana or the Hinayana schools.

There are six significances in the hymns. First, they enable us to know the profound and far-reaching virtues of the Buddha; second, they teach us how to write compositions; third, they ensure the purity of our tongue; fourth, the chest is expanded [while singing them]; fifth, one is not nervous in a congregation [while reciting the hymns]; and sixth, they enable us to live long without illness. After having studied these hymns, one proceeds to learn other scriptural texts. But these fine literary works are not yet introduced to China in the east. There are, however, many expositors of these works; but none of them may really be counted as a sufficiently good poet to write after the same rhymes.

Diṅnāga Bodhisattva personally wrote some hymns of the same caliber in the same style. At the beginning of each verse, he added one of his own, making a total number of three hundred verses, known as the *Composite Panegyric.* A well-known monk, named Śākyadeva of Deer Park, again added one verse before each of Diṅnāga's stanzas, producing a work of four hundred and fifty verses in all, known as the *Mixed Composite Panegyric.* All composers of eulogies take this work to be a criterion.

Once Nāgārjuna Bodhisattva wrote a letter in verse, entitled the *Suhṛllekha,* meaning "a letter to a bosom friend," to his old supporter Jetaka who had the title of Śātavāhana, the king of a great country in the south. The style of the letter is highly ornamental with earnest greetings and exhortations, aiming at the Middle Way as the target of achievement and showing more affection than that shown to a kinsman. The purport of the letter is really manifold. First it advocates respect for and faith in the three honored ones and supporting one's parents with filial piety. One should observe the precepts, relinquish what is evil, and be prudent in choosing friends. The contemplation of impurity should be practiced in matters of wealth and women. One should look after one's household and keep in rightful remembrance that everything is impermanent. One should widely narrate the conditions of hungry ghosts and animals, and describe in detail the affairs of men, gods, and the hells. Even if a fire were burning on the head, one would have no leisure to wipe it out, as one's mind is so deeply absorbed in the truth of the chain of causality in order to gain spiritual liberation. One should diligently practice the three modes of attaining wisdom, and clearly understand the eightfold noble path. It advises us to learn the four noble truths, so as to realize the two perfect virtues. One should be like Avalokiteśvara and make no distinction between friend and foe; then we shall be able to live together with Amitābha Buddha in the Pure Land forever. This is the way to save living beings; no other way is better than this one.

In the five parts of India, all students first studied this letter in verse when they began to receive schooling. None of those who turned their mind [to Buddhism] did not spend their whole lifetimes learning this epistle, just as the monks in China recite the *Sutra on Avalokiteśvara* and the laity read the *One Thousand Character Composition* or the *Book of Filial Piety*. It is universally studied with keen interest. The *Jātakamālā* is a work of the same sort. (Yijing's running note: *Jātaka* means "previous incarnation," and *mālā,* "a collection," i.e., a collection of stories about the hardships the Bodhisattva experienced in his previous incarnations.) If it is translated into Chinese, it would amount to over ten rolls. In order to edify living beings, the birth stories are written in poetry for the purpose of catering to the literary taste of those readers who take delight in perusing fine writings.

At one time, King Śīlāditya, who was exceedingly fond of lit- 228a
erature, issued an order saying, "If any one of you gentlemen has any fine panegyric poetry, show it to us at the audience tomorrow morning." When the metrical compositions were collected, they amounted to five hundred bundles. When the king opened them and read the verses, he found that most of them were adapted from the *Jātaka* stories. From this fact he came to know that these stories were the most excellent writings among all eulogistic works.

On the islands of the South Seas, there are more than ten countries where both monks and laymen chant and recite the above-mentioned eulogistic poems, which are not yet translated into Chinese.

King Śīlāditya also composed songs to glorify the deed of Jīmūtavāhana Bodhisattva, who volunteered to sacrifice himself in place of a serpent. Musicians were employed to play wind and stringed instruments to accompany the singers and dancers, and the songs were thus rendered popular in his time.

Candragomin Mahāsattva of eastern India wrote a song about Prince Viśvāntara, and it is sung with dancing in all of the five parts of India. This prince was formerly known as Prince Sudāna.

The Venerable Aśvaghoṣa also wrote verses as well as the *Sūtrālaṅkāra-śāstra* and the *Buddhacarita-kāvya,* of which the full version, if translated [into Chinese], would consist of more than ten fascicles. In this work, the career of the Buddha, beginning from his life in the royal palace up to his death under the twin *śāla* trees, is told in verse. It is widely read and sung in the five parts of India and in the islands of the South Seas. It is concise in style, but the meaning is clear and the significances, which are manifold, render readers delighted. They never feel bored while reading it. As it conveys the holy teachings, it enables us to gain blessedness and benefits. I am sending home separate copies of the *Hymn of One Hundred and Fifty Verses* and the letter written by Nāgārjuna Bodhisattva, with the hope that those who take delight in reading eulogistic poems will study and recite them.

33. Absurd Ways of Worshiping the Buddha's Image

In our religion there are clear regulations concerning the rites of paying homage. A monk should always exert himself to practice mindfulness during all of the six periods of the day and night, lodging in a single room and living by alms-begging according to the *dhūtaguṇa* (ascetic practices) while cultivating the Way of contentment. He wears only the three robes, without keeping any surplus garments. He should concentrate his thoughts on nonexistence and free himself completely from the encumbrances of existence. Can he now do things in a variant way different from the monastic rules, things such as wearing a monk's robe, and thus not looking like an ordinary man, but worshiping like a layman in the marketplace? When we examine the Vinaya texts, we shall see that such a thing is totally forbidden. The Buddha said, "There are two categories of things that one should worship, namely, the triple gem and senior *bhikṣus*." There are some people who bring the Buddha's image to the highway, where the holy object will be defiled by dust and dirt, in order to get money [from worshipers]. There are some others who bend their bodies, tattoo their faces, break their joints, and pierce their skin, pretending to do so with a good mind, but actually they are trying to earn their livelihood. Such spectacles are never seen in India. I would advise people not to do such things any more.

34. The Ways of Learning in India

The unique voice of the Great Sage embraces all of the three thou- 228b
sand worlds as a whole. It is uttered in accordance with the capacity of the beings of the five ways of existence, by illustrating the seven cases and nine personal terminations [of the Sanskrit language], in order to effect extensive salvation. (Yijing's running note: The seven cases and nine personal terminations of *Śabdavidyā* [the science of words] will be briefly explained below.) There is a store of Dharma, consisting of mental words; and Indra, the Emperor of Heaven, comprehended the inexpressible scriptures. Or the explanation is given in accordance with the usages of grammar in order to enable the people of China to understand the words of the original language, so that those who have cause to read them may develop their wisdom and be gratified, each according

to his own modest mentality, and thereby get rid of defilements in conformity with truth and realize the state of perfect quietude. As regards the supreme truth, it is far beyond the reach of words or speech, but the worldly principles of concealment are not apart from wording. (Yijing's running note: The term "worldly principles" was formerly known as worldly truth, which was not fully expressive of its meaning. The meaning is that ordinary matters conceal truth. The material clay, for instance, is originally not a pitcher, but people erroneously think of it as a pitcher, and in the sound of human voice there is no song, yet people mistake it for the essence of a song. Moreover, when perception arises, its substance is non-distinctive, and it is due to the covering of ignorance that various forms take shape illusorily. Not understanding one's own mind, one thinks that objects exist outside the mind. Both the snake and the rope [that causes the illusion of a snake] are fallacious conceptions. When right knowledge is hidden away, the truth is concealed, and it is thus known as worldly principles of concealment. The word "concealment" implies "worldly," and so we have the term "worldly concealment." Or we may simply say veritable truth and concealed truth.)

But the translators of old times rarely talked about the grammar of the Sanskrit language. Those who recently introduced scriptures into China enunciated only the first seven cases. It was not that they did not know the eighth one (i.e., the vocative case), but they saw no need to discuss it. Now I hope you will all study Sanskrit, so that we can spare the translators the trouble of repetition. Thus I am just writing these paragraphs, merely to give a brief account of the fundamentals of the language. (Yijing's running note: Even in Ku-lun and Suli, the people can read Sanskrit scriptures. Why should the people of the Divine Land, which is a land of abundance, not probe into the original language of the scriptures? In India it is said in praise [of the Chinese people] that as Mañjuśrī is now living in Bing-zhou [in China], the people there are blessed by his presence, and thus they should be admired and praised. The full account is too long to be copied here.)

The *Śabda-vidyā—śabda* means "words," and *vidyā,* "knowledge," i.e., the *Knowledge of Words*—is one of the five treatises. In the five parts of India, secular books in general are known as *vyākaraṇa* (grammar), of which there are five principle works, similar [in popularity] to the *Five Classics* of the Divine Land of China. (Yijing's running note: Formerly it was wrongly translated as the *Pi-qie-luo Treatise.*)

1. The *Siddhavastu* (a spelling book), also known as the *Siddhirastu,* is an initiatory book for beginners in primary school to achieve the aim of gaining good luck in learning. It deals with the forty-nine letters of the alphabet, which are multiplied and arranged in the eighteen sections of a total of more than ten thousand syllables, comprising over three hundred stanzas. There are four lines in each stanza, and each line consists of eight syllables, making thirty-two syllables in a stanza. There are short and long stanzas, and it is impossible for me to give a full account of them here. Children begin to learn this book at the age of six and complete the course in six months. According to tradition it was composed by Maheśvara.

2. The *Sūtra* is the groundwork of all grammatical writings. The name may be translated as "short aphorisms" or explanations of the rules [of grammar]. Consisting of a thousand stanzas, it was composed by Pāniṇi, a great scholar of wide learning, in the old days. He was said to have been inspired and aided by Maheśvara in writing this work, and when he appeared with three eyes, the people of his time believed that it was truly so. At the age of eight, children can complete the study of this *Sūtra* in eight months.

3. The *Book on Dhātu* (verbal roots). It contains a thousand 228c
stanzas especially for the explanation of grammatical roots, and it is as useful as the above work.

4. The *Book of the Three Khilas* (supplementary works). *Khila* means "wasteland"; the metaphor is of the wasteland reclaimed by a farmer. It should be named the *Book on Three Pieces of Desert Land;* namely, (1) the *Aṣṭadhātu,* in a thousand stanzas, (2) the

Muṇḍa, in a thousand stanzas, and (3) the *Uṇādi,* also in a thousand stanzas.

(1) The *Aṣṭadhātu* deals with the seven cases and the ten *la*s (the ten tenses and moods of a finite verb), and also explains the eighteen personal terminations of verbs and nouns. The seven cases are possessed by all nouns, and in each case there are three numbers, namely, singular, dual, and plural. So there are altogether twenty-one forms for every noun. For instance, one man is indicated by *puruṣas,* two men by *puruṣau,* and three [or more] men by *puruṣās*. These forms of a noun are also distinguished by being pronounced in a heavy or a light breath. Besides the seven cases, there is the vocative case, which is the eighth one. As the first case has three numbers, so do the other cases, which are, I am afraid, too complicated to be mentioned here. The cases of a noun are called *subanta,* having twenty-four inflections. The ten *la*s denote the ten grammatical terms [beginning with the letter "l"] by which the three different tenses of a verb are expressed. The eighteen personal terminations indicate the first, the second, and the third persons in the three numbers of a verb to differentiate the worthy and unworthy or this and that. These eighteen terminations are collectively called *tiṇanta*.

(2) The *Muṇḍa* treats the formation of compound words. For instance, the Sanskrit word for "tree" is *vṛkṣa,* with which more than twenty compounds are formed. It is combined with other words to produce the name of another thing.

(3) The *Uṇādi* is roughly the same as the preceding work, except that what is fully explained in the one is only briefly mentioned in the other. Only by studying hard for three years can a ten-year-old child grasp the meanings of these books on the three *Khila*s.

5. The *Vṛtti-sūtra*. This is a commentary of the above-mentioned *Sūtra,* on which quite a number of commentaries have been composed since ancient times, but this is the best one, consisting of eighteen thousand stanzas for the elucidation of the text of the

Sūtra, with a detailed explanation of its manifold meanings, and giving a full exposition of the normality of the universe and the rules of gods and men. A fifteen-year-old child can understand the book after five years' study.

People of China going to India to acquire knowledge must learn this work before studying other books, otherwise they will labor in vain. All these books should be memorized, but this applies, as a rule, only to men of higher talent, while those of medium or inferior capability may pass a test merely by understanding the meaning. They should study hard day and night without any leisure to sleep restfully, just like Confucius, who studied the *Book of Changes* with such effort that three times he wore away the leather binders that strung together the bamboo slips on which the *Book* was written, or like Tong Yu [a scholar of ancient times], who advised his pupils to utilize all their spare time to read books a hundred times [in order to understand them thoroughly]. The hairs of a bull are counted by the thousands, but a unicorn has only one horn. One who has mastered this work is equal in academic rank to the holder of a Master of Classics in China.

This *Vṛtti-sūtra* was composed by the scholar Jayāditya, who was a man of great capability and literary talent. He could understand whatever he had heard once, without having to learn it a 229a
second time. He respected the three honored ones and performed various meritorious deeds. His death occurred nearly thirty years ago. After having mastered this commentary, one may proceed to learn the composition of letters and memorials submitted to emperors, write poems, devote one's mind to the study of the *hetuvidyā* (logic), and pay attention to the *Abhidharma-kośa-śāstra.* By poring over the *Nyāya-dvāra-tarka-śāstra,* one may know how to draw inferences in the right way, and by reading the *Jātakamālā,* one's fine talent may be developed.

After that one receives instructions from a tutor for two or three years, mostly at Nālandā Monastery in Central India, or in the country of Valabhī in Western India. These two places are similar to Jin-ma (the Imperial Academy), Shi-qu-ge (the Imperial

Library), Long-men (the Main Gate of the Imperial Examination Hall), and Que-li (the birthplace of Confucius) in China, where brilliant scholars of outstanding talent assemble in crowds to discuss questions of right and wrong. Those who are praised by wise authorities as excellent scholars become famous for their ability far and near. They may then believe that their sword of wisdom is sharp enough for them to go as competent persons to serve at the court of a king, making suggestions and displaying their knowledge, in hopes of being employed. When they take part in a debate, they always win the case and sit on double mats to show their unusual intelligence. When they carry on arguments to refute [heretics], they render their opponents tongue-tied in shame. Their fame resounds through the five mountains and their repute spreads within the four quarters. They receive feudal estates and are promoted to higher rank, with their names written in white high up on the gates of their houses. After that they may continue to study other subjects of learning.

6. Next, there is a commentary on the *Vṛtti-sūtra,* entitled *Cūrṇi,* consisting of twenty-four thousand stanzas. This work, composed by the scholar Patañjali, makes an analytical explanation of the frame and structure of the above-mentioned *Sūtra* [of Pāṇini], and gives a full elucidation of the latter commentary (the *Vṛtti-sūtra*). In order to understand [Pāṇini's] *Sūtra,* one has to spend three years completing the study of this work, which is similar in merit to the *Spring and Autumn Annals* or the *Book of Changes.*

7. There is also the *Bhartṛhari-śāstra,* a commentary on the foregoing *Cūrṇi,* composed by the great scholar Bhartṛhari in twenty-five thousand stanzas, dealing extensively with the essentials of human affairs and grammatical knowledge, and relating in great detail the causes of the rise and fall of various families. He was profoundly learned in the theories of *vijñapti-mātra* (consciousness only), and was well versed in syllogisms. The repute of this scholar resounded in the five parts of India, and his virtue was known to the remotest frontiers. He had thorough faith in the triple gem and concentrated his mind on the truth of the twofold

voidness. In hopes of gaining the superior Dharma, he became a monk; but as he was much attached to worldly pleasure, he returned to secular life; this he did seven times. If it were not for a deep belief in the law of cause and effect, who could have stuck to the robe as he did so persistently? He wrote the following poem in self-reproach:

> Because of impurities, to secular life I returned,
> Free from desires, the robe again I donned.
> Why do these two mentalities
> Tease me as if I were an infant?

He was a contemporary of the Venerable Dharmapāla.

Once a monk in the monastery had the mind to return to secular life because he was persistently pressed by worldly desires. He asked his pupils to carry him out of the monastery in a sedan chair. When people asked him his reason for doing so, he said in reply, "All places of blessedness are intended for the residence of those who observe the moral precepts. Since my mind is impure now, I am doing wrong to the right Dharma." As he could not find a footing in any monastery, monasteries being for the use of monks from the ten quarters, he became a lay devotee clad in white garments 229b
and then entered a monastery to disseminate the right Dharma. It has been forty years since he passed away.

8. There is also the *Vākya-śāstra* (or *Vākyapadīya*), also composed by Bhartṛhari, in seven hundred stanzas with a commentary in seven thousand stanzas, giving a description of argumentation based on the authority of the sacred teachings and of inference by comparison [as used in syllogisms].

9. Next, there is the *Viṭal(-vṛtta)* in three thousand stanzas with a commentary in fourteen thousand stanzas, the main body of the work being composed by Bhartṛhari and the commentary by the commentator Dharmapāla. This work makes an exhaustive inquiry into the abstruse secrets of heaven and earth and investigates to the utmost the essence of human principles. Only a man whose learning has reached the stage of studying this book

may be said to have mastered the science of grammar and be compared to one who is versed in the *Nine Classics* and the works of all schools of thought in China. All these books must be studied by both monks and laymen; otherwise they cannot win fame as well-informed scholars.

In the case of monks, they should learn all the Vinaya texts and do research into the scriptures and commentaries, so as to be able to defeat heretics in debate, like warriors winning in combat on the battlefield, and to solve queries as ice is melted in boiling water. In this way they become famous in Jambudvīpa and receive more respect than men and heavenly beings, assisting the Buddha in spreading his edification and guiding all living beings [to emancipation]. There may be only one or two such outstanding persons appearing in each generation, and they may be compared to the sun and moon and regarded as *nāga* elephants (the most excellent elephants). In the remote past there were such people as Nāgārjuna, Deva, Aśvaghoṣa, and the like. In the middle ages there were Vasubandhu, Asaṅga, Saṃghabhadra, Bhāvaviveka, and others; while in recent times we have Diṅnāga, Dharmapāla, Dharmakīrti, Śīlabhadra, as well as Siṃhacandra, Sthiramati, Guṇamati, Prajñāgupta, Guṇaprabha, Jinaprabha, and so on. None of these great teachers was lacking in the various religious and secular virtues mentioned above, and all of them were men of little desire, with self-contentment. Nobody could be a match for them. Men of such caliber can scarcely be found among heretics and other secular people. (Yijing's running note: A full account of them is found in the *Biographies of the Ten Virtuous Monks of India.*)

Dharmakīrti reglorified the study of the *hetuvidyā,* while Guṇaprabha popularized the Vinaya texts for a second time. Guṇamati engaged in the practice of meditation according to the School of Dhyāna (mental concentration), and Prajñāgupta made complete distinctions between truth and heresy. They verified that valuable jewels might shine colorfully under the deep blue where the whales lived, and that superb medicines might work wonders on the lofty Fragrant Mountain. From this we may know that the

Buddha-dharma is all-inclusive and nothing is excluded, and that these teachers could write a composition as swiftly as the echo of a sound. They did not need to take the trouble to study the *Fourteen Classics* in full, nor did they need to repeat a book in two volumes a hundred times, being able to understand whatever they had heard once. (Yijing's running note: A heretic composed [a treatise in] six hundred stanzas, and came with them to debate with Dharmapāla, who, having listened to the stanzas only once before the audience at an assembly, committed the verses to memory and grasped their meanings.)

In all the five parts of India, the Brahmans are regarded as the noblest caste. Wherever there is a meeting, they never associate with people of the other three castes, and keep those of mixed caste at a distance. Their sacred texts are the four Vedas, consisting of about a hundred thousand stanzas. The word *veda* means "clear understanding," which in former times was wrongly transliterated as *wei-tuo*. The Vedas are handed down by word of mouth, not by writing them on paper or leaves. From time to time there are intelligent Brahmans who can recite the hundred thousand stanzas. 229c

In India there are knacks for acquiring intelligence. First, by repeated and careful reading, one may gain intellectual power, and second, the alphabet may stabilize the mind. In ten days or a month of practice, one's thoughts will come out gushing like a fountain, and one can understand whatever one has heard once without resorting to a second discussion. As I have seen such men with my own eyes, it is certainly not a falsehood. In Eastern India, there lived a great man named Candragomin, who was a bodhisattva (a being on the way to enlightenment) endowed with great talent and eloquence. When I arrived there, this man was still living. Somebody asked him, "Which is more harmful, passion or poison?" He replied at once, "Poison and passion are really quite different from each other. Poison can harm you only when you take it, but passion will burn you the moment you think of it."

There were also Kāśyapa-mātaṅga and Dharmarakṣa, who spread the good gospel to the eastern capital of Luo-yang, and

Paramārtha, who conveyed the excellent voice to the South Seas. Kumārajīva, the great virtuous one, worked as a master of virtue in an alien land, while Xuanzang, the Dharma teacher, performed the function of a teacher in his homeland. All these teachers, both of the past and in the present, carried forward and spread the light of the Sun of the Buddha. They propagated the theories of both existence and nonexistence, taking the Tripiṭaka as their teacher, and practiced meditation as well as developed wisdom, depending on the *sapta-bodhyaṅga* (the seven requisites for attaining enlightenment) as their master.

There are now living in [Central] India the Dharma master Jñānacandra of Tiladhaka Monastery; Ratnasiṃha of Nālandā Monastery; Divākaramitra of Eastern India; Tathāgatagarbha in the southern borderland of India; and Śākyakīrti of Śrībhoja in the South Seas. (Yijing's running note: He is now living in Śrībhoja. He has traveled extensively in the five parts of India and is well learned.) All of them may be compared with the former wise men in brilliant intellect, and they follow the track of past sages. In understanding *hetuvidyā,* they try to emulate Diṅnāga, and while ruminating upon the theories of the Yogācāra School, they respectfully cherish the memory of Asaṅga. In talking about the doctrine of voidness, they happily coincide with Nāgārjuna, and in discussing the teaching of existence, they have an intimate knowledge of Saṃghabhadra. I had the opportunity to come into contact with these teachers of the Dharma and receive profound instructions from them. I am happy to have acquired new knowledge of what I did not hear before and that I could review my old lessons [through their guidance]. In hopes of transmitting the lamp of truth, I am really glad to have heard the Dharma in the morning, so much so that as my hundred points of doubt were solved like dust being washed away, I would not have regretted it if I were to die in the evening. I was still able to pick up some pearls that were left behind on Vulture Peak and often obtained genuine ones. While I collected scattered jewels in the Dragon River, I came upon the best pieces more than once.

Under the far-reaching protection of the triple gem and with the favor of the Emperor who is a great distance away, I was able to start my homeward voyage to the east. Sailing over the South Seas from Tāmralipti, I arrived in Śrībhoja, where I have been sojourning for four years. I am lingering here without a date on which to come back home.

35. On Keeping Long Hair

To receive full ordination with one's hair kept long is something unheard of in the five parts of India, nor is it mentioned in the texts of the *Vinaya-piṭaka,* because no such thing has happened 230a
ever since ancient times. If a monk had the appearance of a layman, it would be difficult for him to guard against committing faults. If one cannot observe the disciplinary rules, what is the use of accepting them? If a man has the pure mind [to become a monk], he should ask [a teacher] to shave his hair, put on the dyed robe, purify his thoughts, and cherish emancipation as his aim. He should observe the five and ten precepts perfectly. Having received full ordination with a perfect mind, he should practice the rules laid down in the *Vinaya-piṭaka.* After having completed the study of the *Yogācāra-śāstra,* he should then learn the eight branch works designated by Asaṅga. (Yijing's running note: (1) The *Vijñapti-mātratā-siddhi-viṃśatikā-kārikā,* (2) the *Vijñapti-mātratā-siddhi-triṃśikā-kārika,* (3) the *Mahāyāna-saṃgraha-śāstra,* (4) the *Abhidharma-samuccaya-śāstra,* (5) the *Madhyāntavibhāga-śāstra,* (6) the *Pratītyasamutpāda-vyākhyā-śāstra,* (7) the *Mahāyāna-sūtrālaṅkāra-śāstra,* and (8) the *Karma-siddhi-prakaraṇa-śāstra.* Although some works on this list were composed by Vasubandhu, the merits [that they contributed to the Yogācāra School] should be ascribed to Asaṅga.) When a monk has made achievements in the study of the *hetuvidyā,* he should then thoroughly understand the eight *śāstra*s of Diṅnāga. (Yijing's running note: (1) The *Trikāla-parīkṣā-śāstra,*

(2) the *Sāmānyalakṣaṇa-parīkṣā-śāstra,* (3) the *Ālambana-parīkṣā-śāstra,* (4) the *Hetu-mukha-śāstra,* (5) the *Śāstra on the Gate of the Pseudo-cause,* (6) the *Nyāya-mukha-śāstra,* (7) the *Upādāya-prajñapti-prakaraṇa-śāstra,* and (8) the *Pramāṇa-samuccaya-śāstra.*) In studying the Abhidharma (metaphysics), a monk should read through the *Six Pāda*s (the six ancillary works to the *Dharma-saṅgaṇi*), and in learning the Āgamas, he should make a complete investigation of all four of them. He will then be able to subdue heterodox views and defeat heretics, so as to deliberate the right principles for the wide salvation of living beings and give guidance tirelessly to all people. Those who can contemplate the twofold voidness, keep the eightfold noble path in their pure minds, be intent on practicing the four meditations, and strictly observe the disciplinary rules of the seven sections [of the *Prātimokṣa*] for life are monks of high rank.

There are some people who cannot behave in the way mentioned above, but who remain unstained in their private chambers, even though they are living with their families. They are actually living alone in hopes of getting out of the world. They beg for alms to pay taxes to the court, and wear coarse garments just to hide their shame. They observe the eight precepts (Yijing's running note: (1) not to kill living creatures, (2) not to steal, (3) not to engage in sexual conduct, (4) not to tell lies, (5) not to drink intoxicants, (6) not to play music, wear garlands, or use perfume, (7) not to sit on a high or big bed, and (8) not to take food at wrong times) till the end of their lives, with a mind to gain the essential way of getting out of transmigration. And they take refuge in and respect the three honored ones with their thoughts concentrated on the attainment of nirvana. Such persons are next in rank.

There are people who are obliged to live in the confinement of family life, but they support their wives and children, respect their seniors with a mind of veneration, treat their juniors with kind consideration, abide by the five precepts, and always observe the four fast days. (Yijing's running note: On the eighth and fourteenth or fifteenth days of the dark half of the moon, and the eighth and fifteenth days of the bright half of the moon, the eight precepts should be observed; this is known as the "holy practice." If one observes only the eighth precept without keeping the other seven, the merit gained therefrom is very small. The observance of the eighth precept is meant to prevent violations of the other seven precepts and not merely to keep the stomach hungry for no purpose.) They treat others with honesty and sympathy and have the capacity to make themselves be industrious. They live by a faultless occupation in order to pay official impositions. Such people are also regarded as good men. (Yijing's running note: "A faultless occupation" means the profession of trading, as it does not cause harm to living creatures. According to the customs of India, merchants are held in esteem, while farmers are not regarded as important, because the tilling of land involves the killing of living things. Sericulture and butchering, which are causes of deep suffering, injure hundreds of millions of lives every year. When they are practiced for a long time no one thinks they are wrong, but in one's future lives, one will suffer unlimited pains. One who does not follow such occupations is deemed faultless.)

As regards those vulgar people who are so ignorant as not to know about the three refuges and who lead aimless lives without observing a single precept in their lifetimes, unaware that nirvana is a state of tranquility and that birth and death rotate like a wheel, and who always commit sinful deeds, they are in the lowest rank.

36. Disposal of the Property of a Deceased Monk

When it is deemed desirable to divide the property of a deceased *bhikṣu,* a full description of the matter can be found in the Vinaya. I will give a brief account of it here to provide a ready reference in time of need. First of all one should make an inquiry as to whether he had any debts, or he has left a will, and if anyone nursed him

while he was ill. These must be considered according to the law,
230b and nothing contrary to reason should be done. One should know that the remaining things may be disposed of in specific ways.

It is said in the *Udāna* (a section of the Tripiṭaka):

Land, houses, shops, and bedding,
Copper, iron, and leather goods,
Razors, jars, and robes,
Various rods and miscellaneous livestock,
Drinks, food, and medicine,
Beds, seats, and title deeds,
The three precious things such as gold and silver
Either made or unmade into articles,
All those different things
May or may not be divided.
One should know how to differentiate them.
This was told by the World-honored One.

By differentiation, it means that lands, houses, shops, bedding, felt blankets, and copper and iron implements are not to be divided. Among the articles in the last-mentioned category, large and small iron bowls, small copper bowls, door keys, needles, awls, razors, knives, iron ladles, stoves, axes, chisels, etc., together with their bags, as well as earthen vessels, such as bowls, small bowls, *kuṇḍikās* for keeping clean water, oil pots, and pails should be distributed, while the rest are not to be divided. Wooden and bamboo furniture, leather bedding, and hair-cutting tools, male and female servants, beverages and edibles, corn and beans, as well as land and houses, etc., are to be transferred to the community of monks from the four quarters. All movable things are to be kept in the storehouse for the use of monks from the four quarters. Immovable property, such as land, buildings, villages, gardens, and houses, should be transferred to the community of monks from the four quarters. All other things, such as garments, quilts, religious robes, and bathing clothes, dyed or undyed, as well as leatherwork, oil bottles, shoes, footgear, and the like, should be distributed to the monks who are present on the spot. Formerly it was said that a garment with sleeves was not to be divided, but that a white double robe could be divided at one's discretion. Long poles may be used as flagstaffs for hanging streamers before the *jāmbūnada-prabha* image (an image of the Buddha made of gold from the Jambu River). (Yijing's running note: The *jāmbūnada-prabha* image is mentioned in the Vinaya. Its origin is that when the Buddha was not among the assembly of monks, they behaved without strictness and solemnity, so much so that the Elder Anāthapiṇḍada asked permission of the World-honored One, saying, "I wish to make a *jāmbūnada-prabha* image of thee, to be installed at the head of the assembly of monks." The Great Teacher consented.) The slender rods may be used for making tin staffs to be carried by *bhikṣus* while going round [collecting alms]. (Yijing's running note: In Sanskrit a tin staff is called a *hikkala,* representing the sound produced by it. Ancient people translated the word as "tin" because the sound is caused by tin [rings]. It may be called a ringing staff or a tin staff at will. The tin staffs I saw in India have an iron ring on top with a diameter of two or three inches, in which is fixed a bronze tube four or five fingers in length [which produces a sound when percussed]. The staff is made of wood, and it may be thick or slender according to circumstances. It is so long that it reaches the shoulders [when held vertically]. Below the top there is fastened an iron chain about two inches long, the links of which are either round or elliptical. Each link is as large as a thumb and is made by bending a wire so as to let the two ends meet through another link. There are six or eight links in the chain which is attached to the ring on the top. They may be made of copper or iron as one likes. The purpose of making such a staff is to ward off cows or dogs while one is collecting alms. It is not necessary to hold it high in a tiresome manner that fatigues one's mind. Moreover, some people make the whole staff entirely of iron with four rings on top. This is heavy and difficult for one to carry about, and it is very cold for one to hold. This is not in keeping with the original purpose of the staff.)

Among the quadrupeds, such beasts for riding as elephants, horses, camels, asses, and mules are given to the royal household, while cattle and sheep should be transferred to the community of monks from the four quarters and must not be divided. Such ar-
230c ticles as armor and coats of mail should also be given to the royal household, while miscellaneous weapons may be made into needles, awls, knives, and crowns for the tin staffs and then given to the monks who are present on the occasion. (Yijing's running note: If there are not [enough] for general distribution, they may be given only to the senior monks.) Such things as nets are to be made into screens for windows. The best paints and yellow, vermilion, azure, blue, or green dyestuffs are sent to the shrine halls to be used for coloring the images, while red clay and inferior blue substances should be distributed to the monks who are present on the occasion. If wine is nearly turning sour, it may be buried underground, and when it has become vinegar, monks may eat it; but if it is still wine, it should be discarded and must not be sold. The Buddha said, "*Bhikṣu*s, since you have become monks under my guidance, you should not give wine to others nor drink it yourselves. You should not even drip a single drop of wine into your mouths with the tip of a reed." If one leavens dough with wine or distillers' grain, or takes broth prepared with wine lees, one incurs the guilt of transgressing the rules laid down in the Vinaya; one must have no doubts about it. (Yijing's running note: In Ling-yan Monastery, dissolved yeast is often used for leavening dough to avoid the fault of taking wine.) All miscellaneous medicines should be kept in a clean storeroom to be supplied to sick persons when needed. All precious gems, pearls, and jade are divided into two portions, one being used for the Dharma, and the other given to the community of monks from the four quarters. Those for the Dharma are spent for copying scriptures and maintaining the lion seat [used for preaching the Dharma], while the objects for the monks are distributed to those who are present on the occasion. Beds and couches, if inlaid with jewels, should be sold and the proceeds distributed to the monks who are present on the occasion, but wooden

beds should be transferred to the community of monks from the four quarters. All scriptures and their commentaries and annotations are not to be divided, but should be preserved in the scripture library for the common use of monks from the four quarters. Other books should be sold and the proceeds distributed to the monks who are present on the occasion. Those receipts for loans that are claimable at once may be divided right away. If not claimable at once, they should be kept in the monastic treasury, and when the money is reclaimed at a later time, it should be used to replenish the fund of the community of monks from the four quarters. All gold and silver, either wrought articles or unwrought ingots, should be divided into three portions for the Buddha, the Dharma, and the Sangha. The portion for the Buddha should be spent on repairing the Buddha halls and the stupas containing [the Buddha's] hair and nails, and for mending other dilapidation. The portion for the Dharma is used for copying scriptures and maintaining the lion seat. The portion for the community of monks should be shared by them right away. The six requisites of a monk should be given to the person who took care of the deceased when he was on his sickbed. Other miscellaneous things should be disposed of in a suitable way as mentioned above. This subject is fully deliberated in the *Mahāsāṃghika-vinaya*.

37. Use of the Property of the Sangha

At present the clothing of the *bhikṣu*s in all the monasteries in India is provided out of [the storehouse of] the resident monks. The surplus produce of the farms and gardens, or the profits gained from trees and fruits, are distributed to them annually to cover the cost of clothing. One might ask the question: even corn and other foodstuffs left by a deceased monk are transferred to the community of monks, so how can an individual monk share the 231a
beans and millet which are the property of the community? The answer might be that the alms-givers gave up their villages and

manors in order to support the monks. Did that mean that only food was to be provided while they were to be allowed to go naked? In consideration of the practice of providing clothing even to meritorious servants, why should it be unsuitable for householders to do the same [for monks]? If we reason in this way, it is harmless for them to supply clothing as well as food. Such is the general view of the monks of India. However, the Vinaya texts are sometimes explicit and sometimes implicit about the matter.

The monasteries in India possess special farms for their supply of clothing, and the temples in China have their own places from which clothing is obtained. Food is also provided to both monks and laymen. As this is done according to the original intention of the alms-givers, it is logically not wrong for them to partake of the food. All donations of fields and houses and even miscellaneous things are given to the monasteries as a means of providing the monks with food and clothing. There is certainly no doubt on this point. If the original intention of the alms-givers is to give donations for general distribution without restriction, then the alms, though given to the monastery, may be considered gifts for all. Anyone who partakes of the food is faultless because it is what the alms-givers expected beforehand. But in China, monks living independently cannot get clothing from a monastery. Thus they have to work hard to meet their needs, which is really an obstacle in their career [of spiritual cultivation]. Even though they can survive by alms-begging, they are not spared mental or physical exertion. But those who permanently reside in a monastery with food and clothing provided for them may lead a quiet and unperturbed life without going out of the gate of the monastery; then things are much easier for them. Moreover, there are monks who possess only the three robes made of rags, beg food from house to house, live under a tree in a forest, sustain themselves by right livelihood, practice meditation to develop wisdom inwardly so as to fix their thought on the path of *mokṣa* (emancipation), and show kindness and compassion outwardly. One who can lead such a life to his last days is a man of the highest rank.

The property of the community of monks, such as garments, quilts, mattresses, and the like, as well as other miscellaneous articles, should be equally distributed to the monks, but not given to those who live independently. This property should be handled with more care than one would use with one's own belongings. When bigger donations arrive, smaller ones should be picked out and given away. This is the holy teaching expressly taught by the Buddha.

When this property is used in the right way, one will not be guilty or at fault. These things are good enough to nourish one's body, and can spare one the trouble of acquiring sustenance. How can we allow a monastery to be enormously rich, with corn and wheat going rotten in the granaries, male and female servants crowding in the houses, and money and wealth accumulating in the treasury, while the monks do not know how to make use of them but hang together in poverty? What should or should not be done depends upon the discernment of wise people.

There are some monasteries where no common food is supplied, but the monks [in charge of the establishment] divide the monastic property among themselves to prepare private meals to the exclusion of other resident monks. They are the persons responsible for the wrong livelihood of the monks coming from the ten quarters. As they practiced such unlawful deeds of their own accord, who can substitute for them to suffer the painful results in the future?

38. The Impropriety of Self-Immolation

Among Buddhist monks there are quite a number of beginners
who are endowed with a fiercely enthusiastic temperament, but 231b
who do not know how to win the confidence of their predecessors by mastering the sacred scriptures. They think that finger burning is an act of religious valor and that the cauterization of their own flesh is a deed of great bliss. They do such things as they

wish, with the decision made in their own minds. But what is stated in the scriptures concerns the laity, who are exhorted to sacrifice even their own bodies, not to mention their wealth, which is apart from the bodies. Therefore, the scriptures only mention those people who have the mind to do so. No allusion is made to homeless monks, because the monks have to abide by the disciplinary rules of the *Vinaya-piṭaka*. Only conduct which is not in violation of the rules may be considered to be in agreement with the scriptures; if it is against the rules, it cannot be done. Even if the shrine hall is overgrown with weeds, not a single stalk of grass should be damaged; and if a monk is hungry even when he is alone in the wilderness, he should not eat as little as half a grain of rice [at an improper time]. As Priyadarśana was a layman, it befitted him to burn his arms as offering to a Buddha. The Bodhisattva might forsake his male and female offspring, but should a *bhikṣu* try to look for children in order to forsake them as alms? As the Mahāsattva gave his eyes and body, so mendicants were asked to give up their eyes and bodies in alms-giving. Although King Ṛṣisvara once slaughtered [five hundred Brahmans], is that what observers of the Vinaya should do? King Maitrībala sacrificed himself [to feed five *yakṣa* demons], but this is not what monks should do.

Recently I heard that some young people devoted their minds so zealously to the pursuit of the Way that they thought that by burning their own bodies they might attain enlightenment. Thus they made light of their lives and discarded their bodies one after another, not knowing that it is difficult for one to be reborn in the form of man in tens and hundreds of kalpas, and that even if one is born as a human being a thousand or ten thousand times, one may yet be short of intelligence, seldom hearing of the seven *bodhyaṅgas* (the seven requisites for attaining enlightenment) and having no chance to meet the three honored ones.

Now they were born in excellent places and engaged their minds in studying the wonderful Dharma, but they forsook their exquisite bodies too readily after having acquired only one stanza, and turned their corporeal substance into sacrificial offerings, which were not weighty gifts at all, when they had just learned how to meditate on impermanence. They should have persistently observed the disciplinary rules in order to requite the four kinds of favors, and steadily pondered on the gate of meditation so as to free themselves from the three realms of existence. They should have had great apprehension about small faults, just as one protects one's floating bag while swimming across the deep sea, and should have practiced wisdom guarding themselves steadily [against errors], as one takes precautions while galloping on thin ice. Then, with the assistance of friends of virtue, they would have been able to remain composed without fear on their deathbeds with right thought cherished in their minds, wishing to be reborn in the future to meet Maitreya Buddha.

If they had wished to gain the lesser fruition [of the Hinayana], they might have followed the eightfold noble path. Had they intended to learn the greater cause [of the Mahayana], that would have been the commencement of studying it in three periods, each consisting of an *asaṃkhyeya* (an exceedingly large number of) kalpas. But they rashly cut off their lives. I really do not know the reason for it.

The guilt of committing suicide is next only to a breach of the first section [of the four grievous faults] of the disciplinary rules. When I examined the *Vinaya-piṭaka,* I never saw any passage allowing one to commit suicide. For the destruction of passion, the Buddha has personally taught the important method. How can one cut off delusion by burning oneself? The Buddha disallowed castration, and on the other hand he praised those who preserved the lives of fishes in a pond. His golden words forbade us to break the grave precepts at will. It is certainly not the holy teaching of the Buddha to fix our minds on such a practice. But those who practice the Way of the bodhisattva, without restricting themselves by the Vinaya rules, in order to perform self-sacrifice for the salvation of others, are beyond our discussion.

39. The Bystanders Become Guilty

231c Such actions as body burning are manifestations of inner emotions. Two or three intimate friends may work together to instigate neophytes to commit suicide. Those who die first in this way are involved in a *sthūlātyaya* offense (a gross transgression), and those who follow suit will certainly incur the guilt of a *pārājika* (expulsion from the Order) offense, for they refused to live in keeping with the prohibitive rules and wished to die by breaking the precepts. They persisted in [such an evil practice] and never studied the Buddha's teachings. If a monk persuades others to put the idea of suicide into action, he commits a sin that renders him, as the saying goes, as useless as a needle without an eye. If he says to another man, "Why do you not jump into the flames?", he incurs unpardonable guilt, like a broken stone that cannot become intact again. One should be very cautious in this matter.

A proverb says, "It is better to repay the kindness of others than to destroy one's own life, and it is better to foster one's moral character than to defile one's name." It was for the sake of saving living beings from suffering that the Bodhisattva once threw himself down to feed a starving tigress, but to cut one's own flesh in substitution for a dove should not be done by a *śramaṇa*. We are really not of such status as to be put on a par with the Bodhisattva.

I have merely made a rough statement about the right and wrong of this according to the Tripiṭaka. The wise should carefully discern between good and evil. But many a man drowns in the Ganges River every day, and beside the mountain near Gayā, more than one man commits suicide each day. Some people starve themselves and refuse to eat food, or climb up trees to throw themselves down. Such misled people were criticized by the World-honored One as heretics. Some others inflict upon themselves the torment of castration. These actions are deeply at variance with the texts of the Vinaya. When a man was attempting to commit such faults, others, fearing to incur guilt upon themselves, did not dare to dissuade him from doing so. If he lost his life in this way, he lost the great object of his existence as well. For this reason, the Buddha laid down rules disallowing such actions. Men of superior wisdom will never do such things. I shall now relate in the next chapter the traditions handed down by the virtuous ones of ancient times.

40. Things Not Done by Virtuous Monks of Old

As regards my teachers, my personal tutor was the Dharma master Shanyu, and my ritual instructor, the Dhyāna master Huizhi. When I was over seven years old, I had the luck to serve them as their pupil. Both of them were monks of great virtue, living at Shen-tong Monastery, which was built by the Dhyāna master Lang, a sage of the Jin-yu Valley of Mount Tai. Their family ties were at De-zhou and Bei-zhou respectively. The two virtuous monks thought that dwelling in the mountains was good only for themselves; it was not the way to benefit others. Thus they went together to Ping-lin, where, close to a clean brook, they took up their pure abode at Tu-ku Monastery, located some forty *li* to the west of the capital city of Qi-zhou. They used to prepare unlimited amounts of food to make offerings without restriction, and whatever alms they had received they gave away to others with pleasure. It may be said that their fulfillment of the four great vows was as limitless as heaven and earth, and that they practiced the four all-embracing virtues for the salvation of living beings as uncountable as dust and sand. They respectfully constructed temples and performed plenty of meritorious deeds. Now I shall give a brief account of the seven virtues of the Dharma master, [my teacher Shanyu,] as follows:

1. The erudition of the Dharma master. He studied the Tripiṭaka as his major course of learning, but also took an interest in the various schools of thought. He was well versed in both Confucianism and Buddhism, and was perfect at mastering the six

232a arts. As regards the sciences of astronomy and geography, and the crafts of divination and calendrical calculation, he could probe into their mysteries whenever he had the mind to do so. Great was the sea of wisdom in him, with inexhaustible tides flowing out of it. Brilliant was his garden of literary achievements, in which luxuriant flowers always bloomed without fading! His writings, his pronouncing dictionary of the Tripiṭaka, as well as some word books of his, are quite popular in the world. He often said about himself that if he did not know a word, it was not a word at all.

2. The versatility of the Dharma master. He was an expert calligrapher, writing Chinese characters in the smaller *zhuan* style invented by Li Si and also in the greater *zhuan* style originated by Shi Zhou. He was also good at writing the official style used by Zhong You as well as the cursive script shaped by Zhang Zhi. He had as keen an ear for music as Zhong Ziqi, who was able to discern whether Yu Boya was depicting lofty peaks or flowing streams with his seven-stringed zither. He could manipulate the adze as well as the artisan Shi, who wiped away a speck of chalk, as tiny as a fly's wing, dotted on the tip of a man's nose by cutting it with his hatchet without injuring the man's nose. This is what is said, that a wise man is not a utensil [of one purpose].

3. The intelligence of the Dharma master. He could read through the *Nirvana Sutra* in one day, but when he first recited the text, it took him four months to complete the recitation. He did research into the abstruse theories and cleverly probed the mysterious teachings. In educating a little boy, he used to guide him with the doctrines of the Hinayana and was never impatient with him. When he instructed a man of greater intelligence, he would impart all he knew to him as if pouring water into a perfect vessel, with the benefit of offering treasure to his pupil. At the end of the Sui dynasty, as the Way was on the decline [in the region where he was living], he removed to the Prefecture of Yang. When the local monks saw him, they all said that he was a stupid person because he was simple and unadorned in appearance. They asked the Dharma master to read the *Nirvana Sutra*, and appointed

two minor monks to oversee the recitation sentence by sentence. His voice in reading the scripture was grave and cadenced. Between sunrise and sunset, he completed his reading of this text, which was kept in three slipcases. All the people praised and congratulated him at the time, bidding him rest and remarking that it was a rare occasion. All people know about this event; it is not merely my biased eulogy.

4. The liberality of the Dharma master. Whenever he purchased anything in the market, he always paid the price asked by the vendor, no matter whether it was high or low; he never bargained to beat the price down. If a man came to pay off a debt to him, he would refuse to accept the reimbursement. People of his time considered him a man of unsurpassed generosity.

5. The loving kindness of the Dharma master. He attached more importance to righteousness than to wealth and followed the practice of the bodhisattva. He never refused to give anything to one who begged for it. He would give three coins regularly every day as alms to the poor.

Once in a cold month of winter, a guest monk named Dao'an came from a distance in a snowstorm, and both his calves and feet were frostbitten. While he was staying in a village for a few days, his chilblains festered with pus. The villagers sent him to the monastery in a cart. The Dharma master had made a new cape, and when he had just put it on for the first time to go out of the monastery, he came upon the guest monk at the gate and instinctively wrapped the monk's wound with his new cape. A bystander tried to stop him, saying, "You should use some old clothes instead of soiling this new garment." But the Dharma master said, "When trying to aid one who is suffering from bitter pain, the matter is so urgent that no time is left for us to look for anything else." The people of the time who saw or heard about the event praised him highly. Although this was not a very important matter, few people would care to do likewise.

6. The assiduity of the Dharma master. He read through each of the eight versions of the *Prajñā-pāramitā-sūtra* a hundred times

and also recited the whole Tripiṭaka from beginning to end. He exerted himself day and night to practice the essential deeds for
232b being reborn in the Pure Land. He kept the Buddha hall and the monks' abode clean in hopes of attaining the stage of imperturbability. He mostly walked barefoot, lest he should accidentally injure insects. He was never idle in directing his thoughts towards the development of his mind. He swept the shrine hall clean to make it as beautiful as the lotus flowers that unfold to give birth to the beings of nine grades in the Land of Peace and Happiness, and he adorned the scripture chamber as splendidly as Vulture Peak, where four kinds of blooms rained down from heaven [when the Buddha was preaching the Dharma]. All who saw his religious acts could not but praise his merits, which he performed without feeling tired till the end of his life. Besides reciting scriptures, he also chanted the name of Amitābha Buddha. He was always perfect in demeanor whether he was walking, standing, sitting, or lying down, and never idled away a single moment as short as the shadow of the sun moving one inch. The beans used as chips to count the number of his good deeds would make two brimful cartloads, and there was more than one way that he gave extensive succor to others.

7. The Dharma master's precognition of his death. One year prior to his death, the Dharma master collected his own writings and other miscellaneous books on history and piled them up in a big heap, ready to be torn into pieces to be used as mortar for making two statues of the guardian gods in the monastery. His disciples came up and remonstrated with him, saying, "If Your Reverence must use paper, we venture to substitute blank paper [for your writings]." The master said, "My indulgence in literature has led me astray for a long time. Shall I now allow it to mislead others? If I do, it would be like asking someone to drink poisoned wine, or leading someone onto a dangerous path. That is not permissible. If one gives up one's proper duties and devotes oneself to the study of side lessons, one commits a blunder against the Buddha's superior instructions. One must not do to others what

one would not wish others to do to oneself." Then his disciples retired with satisfaction, but he presented them with the *Analytic Dictionary of Characters* and some other word books with the instruction, "When you have just acquired an outline of the classics and history and have mastered a certain number of characters, you should then devote yourselves to the study of the superior scriptures, and must not attach yourselves to such worldly lore and make it a hindrance [to your progress]."

Before his death, the master told his disciples, "I shall certainly be going in about three days, and I shall die with a broom in my hand. My remains should be left in the wide marshland." Early in the morning a few days later, he came to a clean stream. Under a desolate white poplar he walked to and fro beside a cluster of small green bamboos. Then he sat down in solitude and passed away holding a broom in his hand.

When the day gradually dawned, his disciple, the Dhyāna master Huili, came to him in the morning, and was surprised to find that the teacher was silent. He touched the teacher's body and felt that his head was warm while his feet and hands were already cold. Then he wailed aloud and summoned everybody from distant places in the four quarters. The monks wept sadly, in a scene resembling that at Gold River with blood shed on the ground [when the Buddha passed away near the river]. The lay disciples wailed sorrowfully just as when the lustrous pearls broke to pieces on Jade Mountain. They lamented over the early withering of the tree of *bodhi* and sighed with regret that the boat of Dharma should have sunk so suddenly. He died at the age of sixty-three, and his remains were buried in the west garden of the monastery. After his death, he left behind only his three robes, a pair of shoes, and bedding for his daily use.

When the Dharma master died, I was twelve years old. Since the Great Elephant had departed, I had nowhere to go to seek refuge. So I gave up my study of worldly books and devoted myself to the learning of sacred texts. At the age of fourteen, I was admitted to the Order. When I was eighteen I intended to travel to

232c India, but my desire was not fulfilled till I was thirty-seven years old. On the day of my departure, I visited the tomb of my late teacher to pay my respects and bid farewell to him. It was in the season when frosted trees formed a dome over the grave and perennial grasses filled the cemetery. Although the spiritual way separated me from my teacher, I paid honor to him as if he were present before me. Looking around at the place, I made a statement of my wishes to go abroad in the hopes of acquiring merits for the deceased and to repay the deep kindness I had received from my benign master.

The Dhyāna master (Huizhi) paid special attention to the study of the Vinaya and concentrated his mind in meditation. He was diligent in spiritual practice during the six periods of the day and night without feeling tired, and he guided the four groups of devotees from morning till evening, never being fatigued. It may be said that he was even more quiet and peaceful when he was in a boisterous and tumultuous environment, and that he associated with monks and laymen without showing prejudice to anyone. He recited the *Saddharma-puṇḍarīka-sūtra* once a day for more than sixty years, having thus read the sutra over twenty thousand times in all. Although he lived in the turbulent times at the end of the Sui dynasty, when he had to shift from one place to another as directed by fate, he never gave up his mind of reading the sutra. He preserved his six sense organs in purity and maintained the four physical elements in peace and harmony, never suffering from any disease in sixty years. Each time he recited the sutra beside a brook, a parrot would come to stay with him, and whenever he chanted stanzas in the hall, a pheasant inspired by his voice always came to listen to his intonation. He was good at understanding the sentiment of music, and was particularly adept at writing the cursive and official styles of calligraphy. He was inexhaustible in preaching the Dharma to guide others. Although he did not fix his mind on the study of secular books, he was intrinsically talented in understanding them. He composed both the *Stanza on the Six Pāramitās* and the *Liturgy of Making Vows* by lamplight at Tu-ku Monastery.

When he had washed himself clean to copy the *Saddharma-puṇḍarīka-sūtra* with a pious mind, he selected from among the handwriting of famous calligraphers and adopted the best style for copying the scripture. While he was doing so, he kept an aromatic substance in his mouth so as to exhale fragrant breath after having bathed himself clean. Suddenly a *śarīra* appeared on the scripture through his inspiration. When the copy was completed, the title was written in gold on a label pasted on the manuscript, which shone brilliantly together with the silvery characters of the scripture. It was preserved in a precious casket, which was as resplendent as the jade rollers of the scrolls of the handwritten scripture. When the Emperor visited Mount Tai, he came to know about the event and had the manuscript brought to the imperial palace as a holy object for veneration. Both teachers were successors to the late sage, the Dhyāna master Lang.

The Dhyāna master Lang lived during the two Qin dynasties and was well known as a paragon for the five groups of Buddhist followers. Appearing at the gate of each alms-giver, he received offerings from all quarters. Doing things to the satisfaction of the people, he taught them all according to circumstances. For the sake of converting those who are beyond the human world, his temple was named Shen-tong Temple (the Temple of Miraculous Powers). His spiritual virtues are hard for us to understand. His deeds are recorded in detail in a separate biography.

At that time the reigning monarch paid homage [to the Buddha], and his subjects were filled with devotion. When [Lang] had the intention of building a temple, he went into the mountains and encountered a tiger roaring at the Northern River. When he came out of the place, he heard a horse neighing in the Southern Valley. The heavenly well from which water was drawn was never drained away, while the celestial granary which provided rice was always full. Although his divine traces have long been buried in oblivion, his influence remains with us and has not faded away. He, my two teachers, and the virtuous abbot, the Dhyāna master Mingde, were well versed in the Vinaya and grasped the

gists of the scriptures, in which no such practices as finger burn-
233a ing and flesh-cauterization were taught. As instructors of their disciples, they prohibited them from doing such things. I received their instruction in person; it is certainly not hearsay.

We should also carefully observe the deeds of ancient sages and listen to the admonitions of former teachers. Since the time when the white horse [that carried Buddhist texts to China for the first time] was unbridled, and after the blue elephant was unsaddled, Kāśyapa-mātaṅga and Dharmarakṣa illumined the Divine Land as the sun and moon, and Kang Senghui and Faxian served, by their example, as the ford or bridge to the Land of Abundance. Dao'an and Huiyuan crouched like tigers south of the Yangzi and Han rivers, and Huixiu and Fali were like eagles hovering high north of the Yellow and Ji rivers. The disciples of the Dharma followed one after another in succession, with the ripples of wisdom rolling continuously in purity, while laypeople praised and glorified the fragrance of the Dharma without cease. We have never heard that any of them advised others to burn their fingers, nor did we see anyone permitting the practice of cauterizing one's own body. The object lesson is put before our eyes, and it is up to the wise to take it with care.

During spare time in the evening, the Dhyāna master [Huizhi] often sympathized with me in my boyhood and gave me instructions in gentle words. Sometimes he told me stories to divert me from sad thoughts of my mother, as people use yellow leaf of the poplar, saying it is gold, to soothe a crying baby. At other times he spoke to me about the parable of young crows that fed their parents back, advising me to repay the kindness with which I had been brought up. He said, "You must work hard for the continuance and prosperity of the triple gem so that it may be everlasting. You should not indulge yourself in the study of various worldly books and spend your lifetime in vain." As I was then only ten years old, I could only listen to his advice, but could not understand its deep meaning. Whenever I went to pay respect to him in his chamber at the fifth watch early in the morning, he would always stroke me on my weak shoulders with kindness, just like a loving mother fondling her child. Whenever he had any delicious food, he would often not taste it but present it to me. When I asked him for anything, he never denied my request. The Dharma master [Shanyu] was very kind in looking after me, though he acted as a strict father to me, while the Dhyāna master [Huizhi] showed me all the tenderness of a mother. Thus my relationship with my teachers was so perfect that nothing more had to be added to it.

When I reached the qualified age to receive full ordination, the Dhyāna master [Huizhi] was my *upādhyāya* (officiant at the ceremony). After my ordination, one quiet night when he was walking round an image of the Buddha, he suddenly lit incense, shedding tears of emotion, and exhorted me, "It is a long time since the Great Sage entered nirvana, and his teaching is now misinterpreted. Many people take delight in accepting the precepts, but few of them actually observe them. You must be resolute in keeping the major prohibitive rules and never violate the commandments of the first section of the precepts. If you commit the other offenses, I will go and suffer in hell in your stead. You must not burn your fingers, nor should you incinerate your own body."

On the day when the imperial sanction was received, I was happily admitted into the holy Order by the kindness of my teacher. Since then I have devoted myself with utmost effort to the fulfillment of my ambition, not daring to infringe on any of the disciplinary rules. Even a small offense would arouse a great fear in me. In this manner I carefully studied the Vinaya for five years. The Vinaya master Fali's commentaries discussed the deep and abstruse points, while the Vinaya master Daoxuan's writings dealt with the principal gists. When I was acquainted with the judgment of observance and violations of the disciplinary rules, I was asked by my teacher to give a lecture on the Vinaya. While attending his sermons on the *Larger Sukhāvatīvyūha-sūtra,* I begged for my food once a day and always remained sitting without lying down to sleep. Although the monastery in the forest was distant

from the village, I never gave up the practice of alms-begging. Whenever I think of the kind instructions of my great teacher, my
233b tears drop down from whence I do not know.

Hence we realize that when a bodhisattva tries out of compassion to save suffering beings, he is willing to throw himself into the flames of a great fire. When a householder has pity on a poor child [as narrated in the parable mentioned in the *Lotus Sutra*], he peeps in the narrow door of a small cottage. This behavior is certainly not erroneous. As I always attended the master at his feet and never went to any distant place to listen to a lecture, one day he deigned to say to me, "At present I have other disciples to wait upon me. You should not relinquish your studies to stay here for nothing." Thus I traveled with my pewter staff in hand to the region of the House of Eastern Wei, where I devoted myself to the study of the *Abhidharma-samuccaya-śāstra* and the *Mahāyāna-saṃgraha-śāstra*. Then, carrying my satchel with me, I proceeded to the western capital, wherein I began to read and con over the *Abhidharma-kośa-śāstra* and the *Vijñapti-mātratā-siddhi-śāstra*.

Just before I started my journey [to India], I returned from the western capital to my native place to seek the advice of my great teacher [Huizhi]. I said to him, "Venerable sir, as you are getting advanced in age [I should not take a long journey away from you], but I wish to travel far to see what I have never heard before in hopes of gaining great benefits. I dare not make the decision by myself." My teacher exhorted me, "This is a great chance for you, which will not come a second time. Being inspired by your good reasons, why should I cherish personal feelings any more? Even if my spirit is released from existence, I will still be able to witness you transmitting the lamp of Dharma. It befits you to go on your journey at once; you should not linger any more to look back upon things left behind. I shall certainly share with you the joy of visiting and paying homage to the holy places of pilgrimage. As this is an important matter concerning the prosperity of the Dharma, you should make your trip flawless."

Having received my teacher's kind instruction, which I could not disobey, I embarked at Guang-zhou in the eleventh month of the second year of Xian-heng and sailed for the South Seas. Thus I traveled through various countries and arrived in India with my pewter staff. On the eighth day of the second month in the fourth year of Xian-heng, I reached the country of Tāmralipti, which is a seaport of Eastern India, where I stayed till the fifth month, when I resumed my journey westwards with some companions and reached Nālandā and the Diamond Seat. After having worshiped at all the holy places, I came to Śrībhoja before long.

It may be said that my teachers were good counselors who were perfect in continence and chastity as taught by the Buddha, the Tamer of Men. They were born as outstanding model men of their generation to meet the needs of the world. It was under their personal instruction that I was brought up to manhood. That I luckily met these two teachers at the ford to ferry across the river of rebirth was just like having a pilot with good eyesight on a raft for crossing the sea. Since even good deeds and kindnesses done in a small way are glorified with songs and music, why should I not write eulogistic compositions in praise of the great wisdom and benevolence of my teachers?

Here is my poem:

Virtuous are my father and mother,
Who supported me in many kalpas.
When I was in my childhood
They sent me to brilliant teachers.
They ceased loving me with the shedding of tears.
I practiced what I had learned
And depended on virtue and the preceptive rules.
Being illustrious as the two illuminators,
The virtue of my tutors is comparable to heaven and
earth.
They sharpened my sword of wisdom
And nourished my body of Dharma.

They guided and supported me,
Tirelessly giving me instruction
Without sleep even at midnight,
Often appeasing their hunger with a belated supper.
A man of superior virtue shows off no virtue;
That is profound beyond our perception.
They concealed their talents on Mount Tai,
Held their virtues in store in the region of Qi.
Vast was their sea of wisdom,
233c And exuberant their grove of meditation.
Resplendent was their literary genius,
Radiant as the morning sun were their minds in concentration.
A real hard object may be ground but can never be attenuated,
A truly white thing dipped in dark dye is not blackened.
Dying in sitting, my teacher showed a marvelous manifestation,
Inspired by him, wonderfully enough, a pheasant listened to his recitation.
When I was a youngster,
One of them passed away before the other.
I turn the merits of all my good deeds
As perfume to be offered to the deceased.
I repay the kindness of the one who has gone forever,
I requite the grace of the other who is alive but far off.

I wish to meet them at all places so as to prolong our happiness and receive their instruction life after life in order to achieve spiritual liberation. I hope to amass a mountain of well-earned wealth, and devote myself to the practice of pure meditation as calm as a tranquil lake, so that I may be present at the first assembly under the dragonflower tree to listen to the profound sermons delivered by Maitreya (the Buddha to come). While being reborn in all four forms of birth, I should always keep in mind [the achievement of Buddhahood] for fully three long eons.

For fear that my readers should think my words groundless, I will quote here a specimen of the writings of the Dharma master (Shanyu). Once on the fifteenth day of the second month, when all the monks and laymen visited the holy sites of the Dhyāna master Lang on South Hill, my great teacher also went to see the unusual celestial granary and heavenly well, and worshiped at the marvelous holy niche and sacred temple, to which were offered gifts brought from places a thousand *li* away. At that time all of the men of letters under the rule of the Prince of Qi assembled at that place. They were well learned and expert in writing compositions, vying with one another in showing off their literary capacity, and feeling proud of the talent they had. As they wished to have poems written in praise of the statue and the temple of the late Venerable Lang, they recommended that the Dharma master write a verse before the others. Being a competent poet, he did not decline the offer. With an inkslab full of black ink, he wielded his writing brush and composed a poem on the wall in a coherent whole without a break. He wrote the poem with quick movements of the brush in such a consummate manner that not a single word was deleted or changed by marking it out with a dot. The poem reads:

> Glorious and radiant is the light of the virtuous sage
> Whose good counsel over the vast seas spread.
> He lived in an empty valley as his abode.
> An imperial order is treated as a mere vanity.
> Mountains and rivers last through eternity,
> Human affairs change with the changes of time.
> The true state of nonexistence he has attained,
> We can now only see his portrait left behind.

After reading the poems composed by the Dharma master, the scholars were ashamed of themselves, either putting down their writing brushes on pine twigs or casting their inkslabs into a mountain nook. All of them remarked that it was just as when the belle Xishi showed her features and there was no room for the ugly woman Momu to unveil her face. Among a crowd of gifted scholars, none could write a verse to rhyme with the poem. The master's other writings are included in a separate collection.

I, Yijing, respectfully address this letter to the venerable monks of the great Zhou dynasty [at home], from whom I have heard lectures on voidness, or with whom I have discussed the meanings of the Dharma. Some of them have been my acquaintances since the days of my youth, while others became my bosom friends in my middle age. The senior ones have become spiritual teachers, and the junior ones are counted by the tens of thousands.

In the above forty chapters I have only briefly discussed the important points. What I have recorded are the customs practiced by the teachers of India at the present time. What I have written is based on the holy teachings of the Buddha; nothing is out of my personal opinion. Our life elapses as swiftly as a rapid river, and nobody knows in the morning what will happen in the evening. Because I fear that I may not be able to meet and speak to you in person, I am sending you this record before my return. I hope you will make a study of it in your spare time, so that the wish of a man far away from you may be satisfied. All my narrations are
234a made according to the tradition of the Sarvāstivāda School and not of any other sect.

I beg to repeat the following verse:

With respect I have discussed good decorum,
The great and comprehensive counsels.
All being made in agreement with the holy teachings,
I cannot say they are my emotional acquisitions.
For fear we may not meet face to face,
I send you this record in advance.
I hope you will not discard my humble opinions
But will accept my superficial views.
For a hundred generations I followed the sacred traces,
I will sow the seeds of goodness for a thousand years.

My real wish is to make Shao-shi Mountain equal to
Vulture Peak,
And to put the Divine Land on a par with the City of the
Royal House.

End of Fascicle Four

Glossary

arhat: A perfect saint who has freed himself from the bonds of samsara (q.v.) by eliminating all passions. The ideal of the Hinayana.

bhikṣu: A Buddhist monk.

bhikṣuṇī: A Buddhist nun.

bodhisattva: A being who has vowed to achieve Buddhahood someday and who actively engages in the spiritual practices of Mahayana Buddhism to achieve that goal. The chief characteristics of the bodhisattva are boundless compassion for all living beings and clarity of comprehension.

caitya: A shrine.

chauri: A whisk to keep off flies, often used as an emblem of rank.

eightfold path: (1) Right view, (2) right thought, (3) right speech, (4) right action, (5) right livelihood, (6) right effort, (7) right mindfulness, and (8) right concentration. *See also* four noble truths.

five prohibitive precepts: The most serious sins a Buddhist can commit. They are: (1) patricide, (2) matricide, (3) killing an arhat (q.v.), (4) maliciously causing a Buddha to bleed, and (5) causing disharmony in the Buddhist Order.

four nikāyas: Early Buddhist scriptures, divided into four groups, corresponding to four of the five Āgamas of the Pali Canon: (1) *Dīghanikāya,* (2) *Majjhimanikāya,* (3) *Saṃyuttanikāya,* and (4) *Aṅguttaranikāya.*

four noble truths: (1) Life is suffering; (2) defilements are the cause of suffering; (3) all suffering can be ended; (4) the way to end suffering is by following the Buddha's eightfold path (q.v.).

nāga: A serpent deity, a dragon.

nirvana: The final goal of Buddhist aspiration and practice, a state in which all passions are extinguished and the highest wisdom attained.

samādhi: A mental state of concentration and focusing of thought on one object. Also called meditation.

samsara: The world of suffering, death, and rebirth; the opposite of nirvana.

Sangha: In early Buddhism, the community of Buddhist monks and nuns. Later the name was also applied to the whole community of Buddhist devotees.

six arts (of Confucianism): Rites, music, shooting, horse-riding, writing, and mathematics.

six *pāramitās*: The six perfected virtues of a bodhisattva: giving, precept-keeping, patience, effort, meditation, and wisdom.

six ways: The six ways of being considerate or sociable, i.e., being friendly to one's fellow practitioners in thought, word, and deed; sharing one's goods with them; living virtuously; and holding to the truth.

śramaṇa: A Buddhist monk.

ten abodes: The second ten stages of the fifty-two bodhistattva stages.

ten precepts: A novice monk or nun vows to abstain from (1) killing sentient beings, (2) stealing, (3) sexual intercourse, (4) lying, (5) using intoxicants, (6) using bodily decorations or perfume, (7) singing, dancing, or viewing dances and plays, (8) sleeping in a large bed, (9) eating after noon, and (10) keeping money or jewels.

ten stages: The stages of bodhisattva practice.

three divisions: The three categories of the Buddhist canon—(1) the Sutras, the Buddha's sermons, (2) the Vinaya (q.v.), rules of conduct for monks and nuns, and (3) the Abhidharma, commentaries on the Buddha's teachings.

three realms: The rebirth cosmos, which is divided into the realm of desire, the realm of form, and the realm of the formless.

three refuges: The Buddha, the Dharma, and the Sangha. So called because one becomes a Buddhist upon "taking refuge" in them.

three *Yānas*: The three paths to enlightenment, which are (1) the *śrāvaka* vehicle (a *śrāvaka* being a follower of the so-called Hinayana), (2) the *pratyekabuddha* (self-taught Buddha) vehicle, and (3) the bodhisattva vehicle, otherwise known as the Mahayana.

tope: A Buddhist reliquary; a large hemispherical structure enshrining Buddhist relics.

Tripiṭaka. *See* three divisions.

triple gem: The Buddha, the Dharma, and the Sangha.

twelve links of the chain of causality: The twelvefold cycle of causes (*nidānas*) and conditions that make up the human condition, namely (1) ignorance, (2) volitional activity, (3) consciousness, (4) name and form, (5) the six senses, (6) contact, (7) perception, (8) love, (9) attachment, (10) existence, (11) rebirth, and (12) decay and death.

twelve *nidānas*. *See* twelve links of the chain of causality.

Vinaya: Rules of conduct for monks and nuns.

Bibliography

Hazra, Kanai Lai. *Buddhism in India as Described by the Chinese Pilgrims, A.D. 399–689*. New Delhi: Munshiram Manoharlal Pubs., 1983.

I-ching [Yijing]. *Memoire compose à l'epoque de la grande dynastie T'ang sur les religieux eminents qui allerent chercher la loi dans les pays d'Occident, par I-tsing*. Translated into French by Edouard Chavannes. Paris: E. Leroux, 1894.

I-ching [Yijing]. *A Record of the Buddhist Religion as Practised in India and the Malay Archipelago (A.D. 671–695)*. Translated by J. Takakusu. Oxford: Clarendon Press, 1896. Reprint, Delhi: Munshiram Manoharlal Pubs., 1966.

Sen, Surendra Nath. *India through Chinese Eyes*. Sir William Meyer Endowment Lectures. Madras: University of Madras, 1956.

Index

A

Abhidharma 156
Abhidharma-kośa-śāstra 149, 176
Abhidharma-samuccaya-śāstra 155, 176
ācārya 93, 94, 100, 110
acupuncture 119, 120, 125, 126
Āgamas 156
Ājñāta-Kauṇḍinya 9
Ālambana-parīkṣā-śāstra 156
alms 40, 47, 59, 63, 70, 84, 85, 95, 101, 115, 156, 159, 162, 164, 167, 169
  -begging 12, 144, 162, 176
  bowl 28, 32, 54, 72, 77, 78, 93, 94, 96, 101, 111, 116
  -givers 161, 162, 173
  -giving 40, 44, 46, 47, 82, 164
Amitābha Buddha 143, 170
Analytic Dictionary of Characters 171
Ānanda 10
Anāthapiṇḍada 159
Anitya-sūtra 79
antarvāsa. *See under* robe
arhat(s) 10, 70, 91, 101
Āryadeśa. *See* India
Āryamahāsāṃghika-nikāya. *See* Mahāsāṃghika
Āryamūlasarvāstivāda-nikāya. *See* Mūlasarvāstivāda
Āryasāṃmitīya-nikāya. *See* Sāṃmitīya
Āryasthavira-nikāya. *See* Sthavira
Asaṅga 141, 152, 154, 155
A-shan Island 12
Aśoka, King 14, 71
Aṣṭadhātu 147, 148
Aśvaghoṣa 139, 144, 152
Avalokiteśvara 124, 143

B

Bālāha Monastery 63
Banan 13
Bandhana Monastery 37
Bao-fu Monastery 90
bath(s), bathing 43, 44, 66, 79, 88, 93, 102, 103, 104, 122, 127, 135, 137, 138, 158, 173
bed(s), bedding 62, 105, 106, 118, 156, 158, 160, 161, 171
Bei-zhou 167
Bhartṛhari 150, 151
Bhartṛhari-śāstra 150
Bhāvaviveka 152
bhikṣu(s) (*see also* monk) 14, 21, 36, 59, 61, 62, 66, 79, 80, 101, 105, 108, 116, 145, 157, 159, 160, 161, 164
bhikṣuṇi(s) (*see also* nun) 75
Bhojapura Island 12
Bianque 120
Bi-jing 13
Bimbisāra, King 14
Bing-zhou 146
Biographies of Eminent Monks Who Went to the Western Regions in Search of the Dharma 2
Biographies of the Ten Virtuous Monks of India 152
bodhi 51, 171
Bodhidharma 68
bodhisattva(s) 14, 15, 50, 153, 165, 169, 176
bodhi tree 29, 68, 107
bodhyaṅga (*see also sapta-bodhyaṅga*) 164
Book of Changes 149, 150
Book of the Three Khilas 147
Book on Dhātu 147

N

O

W

X

Y

Z

A List of the Volumes of the BDK English Tripiṭaka
(First Series)

Abbreviations

Ch.:	Chinese
Skt.:	Sanskrit
Jp.:	Japanese
Eng.:	Published title
T.:	Taishō Tripiṭaka

Vol. No.	Title	T. No.
11-III	*Ch.* Jên-wang-pan-jo-po-lo-mi-ching (仁王般若波羅蜜經) *Skt.* Kāruṇikārājā-prajñāpāramitā-sūtra (?)	245
11-IV	*Ch.* Pan-jo-po-lo-mi-to-hsing-ching (般若波羅蜜多心經) *Skt.* Prajñāpāramitāhṛdaya-sūtra	251
12-I	*Ch.* Ta-lo-chin-kang-pu-k'ung-chên-shih-san-mo-yeh-ching (大樂金剛不空眞實三麼耶經) *Skt.* Adhyardhaśatikā-prajñāpāramitā-sūtra	243
12-II	*Ch.* Wu-liang-shou-ching (無量壽經) *Skt.* Sukhāvatīvyūha *Eng.* The Larger Sutra on Amitāyus (In The Three Pure Land Sutras)	360
12-III	*Ch.* Kuan-wu-liang-shou-fo-ching (觀無量壽佛經) *Skt.* Amitāyurdhyāna-sūtra *Eng.* The Sutra on Contemplation of Amitāyus (In The Three Pure Land Sutras)	365
12-IV	*Ch.* A-mi-t'o-ching (阿彌陀經) *Skt.* Sukhāvatīvyūha *Eng.* The Smaller Sutra on Amitāyus (In The Three Pure Land Sutras)	366
12-V	*Ch.* Ti-ts'ang-p'u-sa-pên-yüan-ching (地藏菩薩本願經) *Skt.* Kṣitigarbhapraṇidhāna-sūtra (?)	412
12-VI	*Ch.* Yao-shih-liu-li-kuang-ju-lai-pên-yüan-kung-tê-ching (藥師琉璃光如來本願功德經) *Skt.* Bhaiṣajyaguruvaiḍūryaprabhāsapūrva-praṇidhānaviśeṣavistara	450
12-VII	*Ch.* Mi-lê-hsia-shêng-ch'êng-fo-ching (彌勒下生成佛經) *Skt.* Maitreyavyākaraṇa (?)	454
12-VIII	*Ch.* Wên-shu-shih-li-wên-ching (文殊師利問經) *Skt.* Mañjuśrīparipṛcchā (?)	468
13-I	*Ch.* Miao-fa-lien-hua-ching (妙法蓮華經) *Skt.* Saddharmapuṇḍarīka-sūtra *Eng.* The Lotus Sutra	262
13-II	*Ch.* Wu-liang-i-ching (無量義經)	276

Vol. No.		Title	*T*. No.
13-III	*Ch.*	Kuan-p‘u-hsien-p‘u-sa-hsing-fa-ching (觀普賢菩薩行法經)	277
14–19	*Ch.*	Ta-fang-kuang-fo-hua-yen-ching (大方廣佛華嚴經)	278
	Skt.	Avataṃsaka-sūtra	
20-I	*Ch.*	Shêng-man-shih-tzŭ-hou-i-ch‘eng-ta-fang-pien-fang-kuang-ching (勝鬘師子吼一乘大方便方廣經)	353
	Skt.	Śrīmālādevīsiṃhanāda-sūtra	
20-II	*Ch.*	Chin-kuang-ming-tsui-shêng-wang-ching (金光明最勝王經)	665
	Skt.	Suvarṇaprabhāsa-sūtra	
21–24	*Ch.*	Ta-pan-nieh-p‘an-ching (大般涅槃經)	374
	Skt.	Mahāparinirvāṇa-sūtra	
25-I	*Ch.*	Fo-ch‘ui-pan-nieh-p‘an-liao-shuo-chiao-chieh-ching (佛垂般涅槃略說教誡經)	389
25-II	*Ch.*	Pan-chou-san-mei-ching (般舟三昧經)	418
	Skt.	Pratyutpannabuddhasammukhāvasthitasamādhi-sūtra	
	Eng.	The Pratyutpanna Samādhi Sutra	
25-III	*Ch.*	Shou-lêng-yen-san-mei-ching (首楞嚴三昧經)	642
	Skt.	Śūraṅgamasamādhi-sūtra	
	Eng.	The Śūraṅgama Samādhi Sutra	
25-IV	*Ch.*	Chieh-shên-mi-ching (解深密經)	676
	Skt.	Saṃdhinirmocana-sūtra	
25-V	*Ch.*	Yü-lan-p‘ên-ching (盂蘭盆經)	685
	Skt.	Ullambana-sūtra (?)	
25-VI	*Ch.*	Ssŭ-shih-êrh-chang-ching (四十二章經)	784
26-I	*Ch.*	Wei-mo-chieh-so-shuo-ching (維摩詰所說經)	475
	Skt.	Vimalakīrtinirdeśa-sūtra	
26-II	*Ch.*	Yüeh-shang-nü-ching (月上女經)	480
	Skt.	Candrottarādārikāparipṛcchā	
26-III	*Ch.*	Tso-ch‘an-san-mei-ching (坐禪三昧經)	614

Vol. No.		Title	T. No.
26-IV	*Ch.*	Ta-mo-to-lo-ch'an-ching (達磨多羅禪經)	618
	Skt.	Yogācārabhūmi-sūtra (?)	
27	*Ch.*	Yüeh-têng-san-mei-ching (月燈三昧經)	639
	Skt.	Samādhirājacandrapradīpa-sūtra	
28	*Ch.*	Ju-lêng-ch'ieh-ching (入楞伽經)	671
	Skt.	Laṅkāvatāra-sūtra	
29-I	*Ch.*	Ta-fang-kuang-yüan-chio-hsiu-to-lo-liao-i-ching (大方廣圓覺修多羅了義經)	842
29-II	*Ch.*	Su-hsi-ti-chieh-lo-ching (蘇悉地羯囉經)	893
	Skt.	Susiddhikaramahātantrasādhanopāyika-paṭala	
29-III	*Ch.*	Mo-têng-ch'ieh-ching (摩登伽經)	1300
	Skt.	Mātaṅgī-sūtra (?)	
30-I	*Ch.*	Ta-p'i-lu-chê-na-chêng-fo-shên-pien-chia-ch'ih-ching (大毘盧遮那成佛神變加持經)	848
	Skt.	Mahāvairocanābhisambodhivikurvitādhiṣṭhāna-vaipulyasūtrendrarāja-nāma-dharmaparyāya	
30-II	*Ch.*	Ching-kang-ting-i-ch'ieh-ju-lai-chên-shih-shê-ta-ch'eng-hsien-chêng-ta-chiao-wang-ching (金剛頂一切如來眞實攝大乘現證大教王經)	865
	Skt.	Sarvatathāgatatattvasaṃgrahamahāyānābhi-samayamahākalparāja	
31–35	*Ch.*	Mo-ho-sêng-ch'i-lü (摩訶僧祇律)	1425
	Skt.	Mahāsāṃghika-vinaya (?)	
36–42	*Ch.*	Ssŭ-fên-lü (四分律)	1428
	Skt.	Dharmaguptaka-vinaya (?)	
43, 44	*Ch.*	Shan-chien-lü-p'i-p'o-sha (善見律毘婆沙)	1462
	Pāli	Samantapāsādikā	
45-I	*Ch.*	Fan-wang-ching (梵網經)	1484
	Skt.	Brahmajāla-sūtra (?)	
45-II	*Ch.*	Yu-p'o-sai-chieh-ching (優婆塞戒經)	1488
	Skt.	Upāsakaśīla-sūtra (?)	
	Eng.	The Sutra on Upāsaka Precepts	

Vol. No.		Title	*T.* No.
46-I	*Ch.*	Miao-fa-lien-hua-ching-yu-po-t'i-shê (妙法蓮華經憂波提舍)	1519
	Skt.	Saddharmapuṇḍarīka-upadeśa	
46-II	*Ch.*	Fo-ti-ching-lun (佛地經論)	1530
	Skt.	Buddhabhūmisūtra-śāstra (?)	
46-III	*Ch.*	Shê-ta-ch'eng-lun (攝大乘論)	1593
	Skt.	Mahāyānasaṃgraha	
	Eng.	The Summary of the Great Vehicle	
47	*Ch.*	Shih-chu-p'i-p'o-sha-lun (十住毘婆沙論)	1521
	Skt.	Daśabhūmika-vibhāṣā (?)	
48, 49	*Ch.*	A-p'i-ta-mo-chü-shê-lun (阿毘達磨倶舍論)	1558
	Skt.	Abhidharmakośa-bhāṣya	
50–59	*Ch.*	Yü-ch'ieh-shih-ti-lun (瑜伽師地論)	1579
	Skt.	Yogācārabhūmi	
60-I	*Ch.*	Ch'êng-wei-shih-lun (成唯識論)	1585
	Eng.	Demonstration of Consciousness Only (In Three Texts on Consciousness Only)	
60-II	*Ch.*	Wei-shih-san-shih-lun-sung (唯識三十論頌)	1586
	Skt.	Triṃśikā	
	Eng.	The Thirty Verses on Consciousness Only (In Three Texts on Consciousness Only)	
60-III	*Ch.*	Wei-shih-êrh-shih-lun (唯識二十論)	1590
	Skt.	Viṃśatikā	
	Eng.	The Treatise in Twenty Verses on Consciousness Only (In Three Texts on Consciousness Only)	
61-I	*Ch.*	Chung-lun (中論)	1564
	Skt.	Madhyamaka-śāstra	
61-II	*Ch.*	Pien-chung-pien-lun (辯中邊論)	1600
	Skt.	Madhyāntavibhāga	
61-III	*Ch.*	Ta-ch'eng-ch'êng-yeh-lun (大乘成業論)	1609
	Skt.	Karmasiddhiprakaraṇa	
61-IV	*Ch.*	Yin-ming-ju-chêng-li-lun (因明入正理論)	1630
	Skt.	Nyāyapraveśa	

Vol. No.		Title	T. No.
61-V	*Ch.*	Chin-kang-chên-lun （金剛針論）	1642
	Skt.	Vajrasūcī	
61-VI	*Ch.*	Chang-so-chih-lun （彰所知論）	1645
62	*Ch.*	Ta-ch'eng-chuang-yen-ching-lun（大乘莊嚴經論）	1604
	Skt.	Mahāyānasūtrālaṃkāra	
63-I	*Ch.*	Chiu-ching-i-ch'eng-pao-hsing-lun（究竟一乘寶性論）	1611
	Skt.	Ratnagotravibhāgamahāyānottaratantra-śāstra	
63-II	*Ch.*	P'u-t'i-hsing-ching （菩提行經）	1662
	Skt.	Bodhicaryāvatāra	
63-III	*Ch.*	Chin-kang-ting-yü-ch'ieh-chung-fa-a-nou-to-lo-san-miao-san-p'u-t'i-hsin-lun（金剛頂瑜伽中發阿耨多羅三藐三菩提心論）	1665
63-IV	*Ch.*	Ta-ch'eng-ch'i-hsin-lun （大乘起信論）	1666
	Skt.	Mahāyānaśraddhotpāda-śāstra (?)	
63-V	*Ch.*	Na-hsien-pi-ch'iu-ching （那先比丘經）	1670
	Pāli	Milindapañhā	
64	*Ch.*	Ta-ch'eng-chi-p'u-sa-hsüeh-lun（大乘集菩薩學論）	1636
	Skt.	Śikṣāsamuccaya	
65	*Ch.*	Shih-mo-ho-yen-lun （釋摩訶衍論）	1688
66-I	*Ch.*	Pan-jo-po-lo-mi-to-hsin-ching-yu-tsan（般若波羅蜜多心經幽賛）	1710
66-II	*Ch.*	Kuan-wu-liang-shou-fo-ching-shu（觀無量壽佛經疏）	1753
66-III	*Ch.*	San-lun-hsüan-i （三論玄義）	1852
66-IV	*Ch.*	Chao-lun （肇論）	1858
67, 68	*Ch.*	Miao-fa-lien-hua-ching-hsüan-i（妙法蓮華經玄義）	1716
69	*Ch.*	Ta-ch'eng-hsüan-lun （大乘玄論）	1853

Vol. No.		Title	*T*. No.
70-I	*Ch.*	Hua-yen-i-ch'eng-chiao-i-fên-ch'i-chang (華嚴一乘教義分齊章)	1866
70-II	*Ch.*	Yüan-jên-lun (原人論)	1886
70-III	*Ch.*	Hsiu-hsi-chih-kuan-tso-ch'an-fa-yao (修習止觀坐禪法要)	1915
70-IV	*Ch.*	T'ien-t'ai-ssŭ-chiao-i (天台四教儀)	1931
71, 72	*Ch.*	Mo-ho-chih-kuan (摩訶止觀)	1911
73-I	*Ch.*	Kuo-ch'ing-pai-lu (國清百録)	1934
73-II	*Ch.*	Liu-tsu-ta-shih-fa-pao-t'an-ching (六祖大師法寶壇經)	2008
73-III	*Ch.*	Huang-po-shan-tuan-chi-ch'an-shih-ch'uan-hsin-fa-yao (黄檗山斷際禪師傳心法要)	2012A
73-IV	*Ch.*	Yung-chia-chêng-tao-ko (永嘉證道歌)	2014
74-I	*Ch.*	Chên-chou-lin-chi-hui-chao-ch'an-shih-wu-lu (鎭州臨濟慧照禪師語録)	1985
	Eng.	The Recorded Sayings of Linji (In Three Chan Classics)	
74-II	*Ch.*	Wu-mên-kuan (無門關)	2005
	Eng.	Wumen's Gate (In Three Chan Classics)	
74-III	*Ch.*	Hsin-hsin-ming (信心銘)	2010
	Eng.	The Faith-Mind Maxim (In Three Chan Classics)	
74-IV	*Ch.*	Ch'ih-hsiu-pai-chang-ch'ing-kuei (勅修百丈清規)	2025
75	*Ch.*	Fo-kuo-yüan-wu-ch'an-shih-pi-yen-lu (佛果圜悟禪師碧巖録)	2003
	Eng.	The Blue Cliff Record	
76-I	*Ch.*	I-pu-tsung-lun-lun (異部宗輪論)	2031
	Skt.	Samayabhedoparacanacakra	
76-II	*Ch.*	A-yü-wang-ching (阿育王經)	2043
	Skt.	Aśokarāja-sūtra (?)	
	Eng.	The Biographical Scripture of King Aśoka	

Vol. No.		Title	T. No.
76-III	*Ch.*	Ma-ming-p'u-sa-ch'uan （馬鳴菩薩傳）	2046
76-IV	*Ch.*	Lung-shu-p'u-sa-ch'uan （龍樹菩薩傳）	2047
76-V	*Ch.*	P'o-sou-p'an-tou-fa-shih-ch'uan （婆藪槃豆法師傳）	2049
76-VI	*Ch.*	Pi-ch'iu-ni-ch'uan （比丘尼傳）	2063
76-VII	*Ch.*	Kao-sêng-fa-hsien-ch'uan （高僧法顯傳）	2085
76-VIII	*Ch.*	Yu-fang-chi-ch'ao: T'ang-ta-ho-shang-tung-chêng-ch'uan （遊方記抄: 唐大和上東征傳）	2089-(7)
77	*Ch.*	Ta-t'ang-ta-tz'ŭ-ên-ssŭ-san-ts'ang-fa-shih-ch'uan （大唐大慈恩寺三藏法師傳）	2053
	Eng.	A Biography of the Tripiṭaka Master of the Great Ci'en Monastery of the Great Tang Dynasty	
78	*Ch.*	Kao-sêng-ch'uan （高僧傳）	2059
79	*Ch.*	Ta-t'ang-hsi-yü-chi （大唐西域記）	2087
	Eng.	The Great Tang Dynasty Record of the Western Regions	
80	*Ch.*	Hung-ming-chi （弘明集）	2102
81–92	*Ch.*	Fa-yüan-chu-lin （法苑珠林）	2122
93-I	*Ch.*	Nan-hai-chi-kuei-nei-fa-ch'uan （南海寄歸内法傳）	2125
	Eng.	Buddhist Monastic Traditions of Southern Asia	
93-II	*Ch.*	Fan-yü-tsa-ming （梵語雑名）	2135
94-I	*Jp.*	Shō-man-gyō-gi-sho （勝鬘經義疏）	2185
94-II	*Jp.*	Yui-ma-kyō-gi-sho （維摩經義疏）	2186
95	*Jp.*	Hok-ke-gi-sho （法華義疏）	2187
96-I	*Jp.*	Han-nya-shin-gyō-hi-ken （般若心經秘鍵）	2203
96-II	*Jp.*	Dai-jō-hos-sō-ken-jin-shō （大乘法相研神章）	2309
96-III	*Jp.*	Kan-jin-kaku-mu-shō （觀心覺夢鈔）	2312

Vol. No.		Title	*T*. No.
97-I	*Jp.*	Ris-shū-kō-yō（律宗綱要）	2348
	Eng.	The Essentials of the Vinaya Tradition	
97-II	*Jp.*	Ten-dai-hok-ke-shū-gi-shū（天台法華宗義集）	2366
	Eng.	The Collected Teachings of the Tendai Lotus School	
97-III	*Jp.*	Ken-kai-ron（顯戒論）	2376
97-IV	*Jp.*	San-ge-gaku-shō-shiki（山家學生式）	2377
98-I	*Jp.*	Hi-zō-hō-yaku（秘藏寶鑰）	2426
98-II	*Jp.*	Ben-ken-mitsu-ni-kyō-ron（辨顯密二教論）	2427
98-III	*Jp.*	Soku-shin-jō-butsu-gi（即身成佛義）	2428
98-IV	*Jp.*	Shō-ji-jis-sō-gi（聲字實相義）	2429
98-V	*Jp.*	Un-ji-gi（吽字義）	2430
98-VI	*Jp.*	Go-rin-ku-ji-myō-hi-mitsu-shaku（五輪九字明秘密釋）	2514
98-VII	*Jp.*	Mitsu-gon-in-hotsu-ro-san-ge-mon（密嚴院發露懺悔文）	2527
98-VIII	*Jp.*	Kō-zen-go-koku-ron（興禪護國論）	2543
98-IX	*Jp.*	Fu-kan-za-zen-gi（普勧坐禪儀）	2580
99–103	*Jp.*	Shō-bō-gen-zō（正法眼藏）	2582
104-I	*Jp.*	Za-zen-yō-jin-ki（坐禪用心記）	2586
104-II	*Jp.*	Sen-chaku-hon-gan-nen-butsu-shū（選擇本願念佛集）	2608
	Eng.	Senchaku Hongan Nembutsu Shū	
104-III	*Jp.*	Ris-shō-an-koku-ron（立正安國論）	2688
104-IV	*Jp.*	Kai-moku-shō（開目抄）	2689
104-V	*Jp.*	Kan-jin-hon-zon-shō（觀心本尊抄）	2692
104-VI	*Ch.*	Fu-mu-ên-chung-ching（父母恩重經）	2887

Vol. No.		Title	T. No.
105-I	*Jp.*	Ken-jō-do-shin-jitsu-kyō-gyō-shō-mon-rui (顯淨土眞實教行証文類)	2646
105-II	*Jp.*	Tan-ni-shō (歎異抄)	2661
	Eng.	Tannishō: Passages Deploring Deviations of Faith	
106-I	*Jp.*	Ren-nyo-shō-nin-o-fumi (蓮如上人御文)	2668
	Eng.	Rennyo Shōnin Ofumi: The Letters of Rennyo	
106-II	*Jp.*	Ō-jō-yō-shū (往生要集)	2682
107-I	*Jp.*	Has-shū-kō-yō (八宗綱要)	蔵外
	Eng.	The Essentials of the Eight Traditions	
107-II	*Jp.*	San-gō-shī-ki (三教指帰)	蔵外
107-III	*Jp.*	Map-pō-tō-myō-ki (末法燈明記)	蔵外
	Eng.	The Candle of the Latter Dharma	
107-IV	*Jp.*	Jū-shichi-jō-ken-pō (十七條憲法)	蔵外